Foreign Investment and Regional Development

G. Richard Thoman

The Praeger Special Studies program—
utilizing the most modern and efficient book
production techniques and a selective
worldwide distribution network—makes
available to the academic, government, and
business communities significant, timely
research in U.S. and international economic, social, and political development.

Foreign Investment and Regional Development
The Theory and Practice of Investment Incentives, with a Case Study of Belgium

Praeger Publishers New York Washington London

PRAEGER SPECIAL STUDIES IN INTERNATIONAL ECONOMICS AND DEVELOPMENT

PRAEGER PUBLISHERS
111 Fourth Avenue, New York, N.Y. 10003, U.S.A.
5, Cromwell Place, London S.W.7, England

Published in the United States of America in 1973
by Praeger Publishers, Inc.

All rights reserved

© 1973 by Praeger Publishers, Inc.

Library of Congress Catalog Card Number: 72-85978

Printed in the United States of America

ACKNOWLEDGMENTS

The author wishes to thank all those persons who contributed their time and encouragement to this work. Particular thanks go to Professors Don H. Humphrey and Henri Schwamm; also Professors George Halm, W. S. Barnes, W. S. Surrey, Warten Law, and Jean Boddewyn. Mr. Charles Van Overstraeten of the Belgian Consulate in New York provided documentation and helpful interpretation. My gratitude also goes to professional colleagues in the Treasurer's Department of Esso International: C. P. Cormier, W. F. Leany, A. H. Wofford, T. L. Thompson, B. F. Havell, M. D. Moore, and M. L. Laflin; to D. McDermott, F. G. Weiss, and T. O. Homan of Standard Oil (New Jersey); and to D. V. Potter of Esso Europe Treasurer's Department, who patiently taught me the realities of international finance. At McKinsey and Company, Lou Gerstner, John Wooster and Bob Schmitz have provided assistance and encouragement for this book. To Mr. and Mrs. Donald R. MacJanet, appreciation for their friendship and guidance; and finally and most importantly, to my partner in every aspect of this study, Wenke B. Thoman.

CONTENTS

LIST OF TABLES AND FIGURES

TABLES IN THE APPENDIX

LIST OF FIGURES

xi

INTRODUCTION

The purpose of this study is to inquire into the nature and effectiveness of investment incentive programs designed to attract foreign investors into depressed areas of developed host countries. The primary questions that will be examined are (1) the economic characteristics of industries that locate in depressed areas and (2) a consideration of the most effective types of incentives.

The study was motivated by an interest in both regional development problems and foreign investment. Association with a consulting project on regional development problems in Canada followed by a brief fellowship at the Common Market Headquarters in Brussels studying foreign investment patterns in Europe made it apparent to me that these two interests could be fruitfully combined. Regional development problems were assuming an increasingly high priority in many developed countries and foreign investment was playing an important role in the depressed area programs, but further research indicated that very little work had been done in monitoring the depressed area programs. The programs were generally set up with certain target goals, but there appeared to be little follow-up research into the types of foreign investment attracted by the incentives and how the economic characteristics of these types related to the government's regional development goals. In addition, there was little available work concerning the effectiveness of the various types of incentives that were offered by host governments. In benefit-cost terminology this study may be viewed as an effort to focus more clearly on both the economic characteristic of the firms attracted to the depressed areas (their benefit to the host country) and the effectiveness of the various types of incentive (the cost to the host country). In addition, I thought it would be useful, drawing on my industrial experience, to include a chapter concerned with how the foreign investor evaluates the types of investment incentives.

The methodology of this volume is to study one investment incentive program in detail and then to apply the conclusions derived from this case to investment incentive programs in other developed countries. The case selected is that of the Belgian investment incentive program offered in the Law of July 14, 1966 (and in effect until December 31, 1970), and was selected because of its success in attracting foreign investment.

The book is divided into two parts. Part I, containing Chapters 1, 2, and 3, is an in-depth study of the Belgian investment incentive program. Chapter 1 is a brief introduction to Belgian Economic structure and to the regional problems that created the need for an investment incentive program to promote regional development. Chapter 2 is a fairly detailed consideration of the various investment incentive laws, culminating with the 1966 Law, that were enacted by the Belgian government to deal with the regional and sectoral problems that were described in Chapter 1. Chapter 3 discusses the reaction by foreign investors to the 1966 incentive Law. This is an extended attempt, based largely on original research, to determine the economic characteristics of industries that have a high tendency to invest in the depressed areas and the effects of these industrial characteristics on the regional development process. Finally, the results of the program are compared with its aims as expressed in the 1966 Law, and conclusions are drawn concerning the various components of a successful investment incentive program for regional development within the Belgian context.

Part II, consisting of Chapters 4, 5, 6, and 7, is an attempt to extend certain of the conclusions reached with regard to Belgium to other developed countries. Chapter 4 considers the role of the investment incentive in the overall process of resource allocation. It provides a basis for understanding why subsidies are given and the type of analysis that should go into deciding the size of the incentive. Chapter 5 suggests certain improvements in the Belgian depressed area program that are also applicable to other developed countries. The method is to summarize the costs and benefits for an individual international firm locating in a depressed region. This discussion of the theory of the firm leads to a more precise discussion of the value of various types of incentives from the point of view of both the host government and the investor. The chapter concludes with a consideration of the extent to which conclusions reached with regard to Belgian depressed areas might have broader applications in depressed area programs of other developed countries. Chapter 6 considers the methods by which the foreign investor should analyze the relative attractiveness of depressed area location. This is the converse case to that of Chapter 5, which concentrates on the viewpoint of the host government. The chapter shows how to calculate the true value or subsidy component of direct capital grants, low-interest loans, and accelerated depreciation allowances. Chapter 7 presents a general conclusion to the study.

The Appendix is an econometric treatment of the variables determining the value of U.S. direct investment in the European Economic Community (EEC), including the use of new variables and the criticism of previous empirical work done in this area.

I

A SUCCESSFUL
INVESTMENT INCENTIVE
PROGRAM:
A CASE STUDY
OF BELGIUM

1

BELGIAN
ECONOMIC HISTORY,
INDUSTRIAL STRUCTURE,
AND REGIONAL DEVELOPMENT

INTRODUCTION

This chapter will provide a brief discussion of the Belgian industrial structure and the development of regional depressed areas. The chapter is divided into two principal sections: the first, a study of contemporary Belgian industrial structure, focuses on the changes in the economy as a result of the Common Market and the role of foreign investment in these changes; the second is a consideration of the regional implications of the change in the Belgian industrial structure. This is intended as a direct link to comprehension of the need for the government's regional development program and of certain of the economic factors underlying that need.

BELGIAN INDUSTRIAL STRUCTURE

Domestic Economy

In the decade from 1958 to 1968 the Belgian government attempted to encourage the installation of modern industries that would update the country's industrial structure and enable it to compete more effectively with Common Market partners and with international producers of competitive products who benefited from lower domestic costs. The result of this policy, combined with investment creation in the Common Market was to precipitate a large flow of foreign (primarily American) investment into Belgium.[1] The index of book value of American direct investment in Belgium was 968 in 1970 (1957 = 100). Other comparable figures for Belgium's neighbors are Britain 422, France 566, Italy 653, and the Netherlands 702, while the overall index for all Western Europe was 613.[2]

The increase in Belgian GNP (gross national product) was stimu-
lated by the inflow of foreign capital. In both real and market terms
Belgium had one of the fastest growing economies in the Common
Market by the middle of the 1960s. By mid-1964 the beginnings of
severe (for Belgium) inflationary pressures induced the government
to restrict the growth of the economy. Table 1 illustrates the market
rate of growth, the real rate of growth, and the rate of inflation for
Belgium for the period 1959-70.

The Belgian population growth rate remained small during the
1960s relative to most of the developed world. In particular, during
the period from 1962 to 1970 the Belgian population increased from
9.22 million to 9.69 million, a compound rate of increase of only .9
percent annually.[3] The three major Common Market countries increased at rates just over 1 percent annually, while the Netherlands
was growing at 1.1 percent annually. The rapidly rising GNP of Belgium, combined with its lower population growth rate, meant that,
relative to its European neighbors, Belgian GNP per capita increased
even more rapidly during this period than its GNP.

TABLE 1

Rates of Growth of Belgian GNP
in Real and Market Terms, 1959-70
(in percent)

Year	Rate of Growth in GNP at Market Prices	GNP Rate of Growth in Real Terms	Price Changes
1959	2.3	(2.2)	4.5
1960	6.5	4.3	2.2
1961	5.9	2.1	3.8
1962	6.9	3.1	3.7
1963	7.7	2.0	5.7
1964	12.0	6.8	5.2
1965	9.1	3.8	5.3
1966	7.5	3.0	4.5
1967	7.1	3.9	3.2
1968	6.3	3.5	3.8
1969	10.9	6.8	4.1
1970	11.5	6.1	5.4

Source: Bulletin d'Information et de Documentaire, National
Bank of Belgium, April 1969 and November 1971.

FIGURE 1

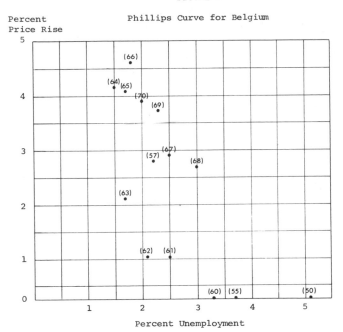

Percent
Price Rise   Phillips Curve for Belgium

Percent Unemployment

Source: Institut National de Statistique, Annuaire Statistique de la Belgique 1970 (Brussels: Ministry of Economic Affairs) and L'Economie Belge en 1970 (Brussels: Ministry of Economic Affairs); National Bank of Belgium, Bulletin de la Banque National de Belgique, II, No. 5 (November 1971).

The unemployment problem that had been the greatest Belgian social and economic problem during the 1950s was reduced. The twin problems of low domestic demand and slow economic growth combined with large unemployment resulting from the declining industries of coal and textiles were overcome by the domestic expansion of the early 1960s. A Phillip's curve for Belgium, which is plotted in Figure 1, indicates that there has been a change in the relation between unemployment and price increases. The curve seems to be moving to the left on the employment axis, so that although the correlation between unemployment and price increases is not high (-.29) for the entire 1950-70 period, the correlations between prices

TABLE 2

Gross Fixed Capital Expenditure (excluding
residential construction) as a Percentage of GNP, 1958-70

Year	Percent
1948-57 average	11.3
1958-67 average	14.8
1958	12.0
1959	12.5
1960	13.3
1961	15.0
1962	15.8
1963	15.8
1964	16.8
1965	15.5
1966	16.9
1967	15.8
1968	16.5
1969	17.3
1970	17.5

Source: Calculated from Bulletin d'Information et de Documentaire, National Bank of Belgium, November 1971, Table I = 4a, Composition of National Product.

and unemployment in the later periods is higher ($r = -.57$ for 1964-
70).*
    The role of foreign investment in the growth of the Belgian
economy can be illustrated by a discussion of capital formation and
foreign investment. One characteristic of the Belgian economy of the
1950s was its extremely low rate of capital formation. The changes
in the rate of capital formation are shown in Table 2.

---

    *The analytical use of the Phillip's curve is limited to an extent
in the Belgian case because of monopoly and monopsony forces in the
marketplace. Belgian industrial structure has traditionally been controlled by large holding companies such as Societe Generale. On the
supply side of the labor curve, 56 percent of the total labor force in
Belgium are union members, the highest percentage of any developed
country. Other similar percentages are Britain 40 percent, Italy

This allocation of a constantly larger share of a constantly larger pie to capital formation is without historical precedent in recent Belgian economic history. Moreover, it appears that much of the increase in the rate is due to foreign investment, either in the form of imported capital or of domestic capital utilized by foreign firms.[4] By the author's calculations, complemented by estimates of other sources, approximately 20 percent of the total gross industrial capital formation in Belgium in 1965 and 1966 was made by foreign investors.[5]

In addition to the macroeconomic growth effects of foreign investment, the capital inflow also changed the sectorial structure of Belgian industry. An examination of the contributions by sector to Belgian industrial production reveals some important modifications. The declining industries of coal and textiles contributed significantly less to total industrial production in 1967 than they had eleven years previously. The vulnerable homogeneous product industries of basic metals and metallic fabrications declined in importance from 47.3 percent of total industrial production in 1956 to 31.3 percent in 1967. Conversely, the more profitable sectors such as chemicals, petroleum, and foods comprised a larger portion of total production in 1967 than they did in 1956. The food, beverage, and tobacco industry expanded greatly during this period, reflecting large American investments.[6] Chemicals, petroleum, plastics, and electronics also achieved large increases in their share of total Belgian industrial production.[7] The share of total industrial production by sector are summarized in Table 3.

One of the most auspicious trends in the Belgian economy in the period 1958-70 was the improvement in corporate profitability. Low profit margins had been the primary cause of the low rate of Belgian capital formation in the 1946-58 period. Alexandre Lamfalussy, in his study of defensive investment in Belgium, has calculated that between 1948-56 approximately 50 percent of the industrial investment was made in sectors with a historic return under the normal profit levels, 25 percent were borderline cases between defensive and enterprise investment, and only the remaining 25 percent was pure enterprise investment.[8]

The improved profit margins in the years 1958-70 are a result of two factors. The first is the smaller allocation of resources to sectors of low profitability. The allocation of larger resources to more profitable sectors naturally raises the average profitability figure. The second factor was the growth of Belgian internal demand

35 percent, United States 22 percent, Germany 26 percent, and the Netherlands 27 percent. See The Economist, October 26, 1968, pp. 13 and 75 of the special section on the Benelux countries.

TABLE 3

Total Industrial Production by Sector, 1956 and 1970
(in percent)

	1956	1970
Mining and quarrying	15.3	2.4
Gas, electricity, and water	2.5	7.1
Food, beverage, and tobacco	6.9	17.3
Textiles	13.7	6.0
Basic metals	15.0	10.3
Metal products	32.3	29.8
Chemicals	5.6	6.9
Others	8.7	20.2
Total industrial production	100.0	100.0

Sources: 1956 figures: Industrial Statistics, O.E.E.C., Paris, 1958, p. 4, 1967 figures: Bulletin d'information et de Documentation, National Bank of Belgium, Table I-3, GNP. Calculated by analysis of national production at market prices.

in the 1960-64 period that provided more profitable domestic sales opportunities than were normally provided on the highly competitive export market.[9] The profit figures for the 1948-56 period and for the 1959-69 period are compared in Table 4.

This table seems to suggest that the defensive investment phenomenon discussed by Lamfalussy still exists today in Belgium but is mitigated by the relatively smaller investments in defensive sectors. Profits of the defensive sectors were relatively lower compared with the national average in 1959-67 than in 1948-56. The return on investment in the textile industry was 2.0 percentage points lower than the national average for 1948-56. In the 1959-69 period the return was 3.7 percentage points lower. In the coal sector the situation was even worse, with the investment return 8.8 percentage points under the Belgian average in the 1948-56 period and 11.8 percentage points under it during 1957-69. This analysis indicates that although fewer resources were being allocated to the defensive sectors, the value of a unit of resources so allocated would be less than it was ten to fifteen years ago.

TABLE 4

Comparison of Profit Margins by Industry, 1959-69*

Years	Total Industry	Chemi-cals	Food and Beverage	Tex-tiles	Coal
1948-56 average	5.8	11.4	6.0	3.8	-3.0
1959-69 average	6.7	7.0	7.5	3.0	-5.1
1959	5.8	5.5	7.3	.5	-3.3
1960	7.0	7.1	8.0	3.8	-7.1
1961	7.3	6.6	7.4	4.4	-11.9
1962	7.7	7.3	8.4	3.6	-5.8
1963	7.0	7.2	8.0	3.1	- .4
1964	6.8	7.9	6.5	4.2	.8
1965	7.0	8.9	7.3	3.2	-4.9
1966	6.8	8.2	7.2	2.3	-4.3
1967	5.3	6.4	7.7	2.4	-8.2
1968	5.5	5.2	8.3	1.4	-6.3
1969	6.6	6.8	6.7	4.2	-4.2

*Profit is defined as return on invested capital and reserves.

Sources: 1948-56: calculated from Alexandre Lamfalussy, Investment and Growth in Mature Economics (New York: Macmillan, 1961), p. 131. The total industry figure is the average for the industries that Lamfalussy graphs for the period, weighted by their size of investment.

1959-69: from L'Economie Belge en 1970 (Brussels: Ministry of Economic Affairs), pp. 306-7. Percentage return on investment calculated by author.

Belgium has a relatively efficient capital market. In a study of European capital markets, the usage of external long-term funding by Belgian companies compares favorably with the U.S. companies for the same year. For a sample of 286 Belgian companies in 1964, internally generated funds (depreciation and retained earnings) accounted for 49.1 percent of total sources of funds; increases on external long-term liabilities were 15.3 percent, with 13.2 percent of the total sources being obtained by the sale of equity. The remaining 22.4 percent was increases in short-term liabilities. In 1963 the combined increase in equity and long-term liabilities was 17.5 percent of total sources.[10] In the United States in the same period 68 percent

of total sources of funds was obtained from operations (profits plus
depreciation), and another 18 percent came from the sale of equity
(5.8 percent) or the increase in long-term debt (12.2 percent).[11] This
recourse to external long-term funding in the United States in 1964
is slightly higher than the 1963 Belgian figure (18 percent versus 17.5
percent) but considerably lower than the 1964 Belgian figure (18 percent versus 25 percent).

The conclusion concerning comparative corporate funding between
the United States and Belgium is that the capital market has compensated for the lack of internally generated funds by the Belgian firms
in extending short-term liabilities and a greater amount of term debt
and equity financing than one would have thought possible. The relative
liquidity of the Belgian debt market combined with its traditionally
low rates provides an extra incentive to prospective foreign investment.

International Aspects of the Belgian Economy

Belgium has been and still is an extremely open economy. The
country benefited greatly from the large increase in world trade in
the 1950s and the 1960s. The effect of this was to increase the share
of its exports as a percent of GNP from 29 percent in 1958 to 43.5
percent in 1970, which means that Belgium is one of the most open
economies in the developed world.[12] The most important changes
have been in the structure of foreign trade and in its geographic dispersion, reflecting the trade creation and diversion effects of the
Common Market.

The structure of Belgian exports has changed almost as rapidly
as has the domestic industrial structure. Many exports are still in
homogeneous product industries that are vulnerable to foreign competition. The demand for these depends upon excess domestic demand
in the importing country as well as export competitiveness of Belgian
products. The share of exports accounted for by the homogeneous
product industries (textiles, metallic ores, and bare metals industries)
has fallen from a total of 49.4 percent in 1956 to 32.9 percent in 1968.
This relative drop has been compensated for by increases in the
share of product differentiated industries such as machinery and
equipment, motor vehicles, and other industry categories including
foods and plastics. These proportionate shares are illustrated in
Table 5.

The changes in geographic dispersion of Belgian exports are
primarily a result of the trade creation and diversion effects of the
Common Market.[13] The total share of Belgian exports taken by the
other four members of the Common Market has risen from 45.2

TABLE 5

Exports as a Percent of Industrial Products, 1956 and 1970

Sector	1956	1970
Steel and semi-finished steel products	33.2	16.8
Textiles	19.2	11.4
Machinery and equipment	8.7	14.8
Motor vehicles	5.9	9.2
Nonferrous metal manufacturing	3.9	7.9
Chemicals	9.7	8.4
Construction material	4.4	.2
Others*	15.0	31.3
Totals	100.0	100.0

Sources: 1956 figures: Alexandre Lamfalussy, Investment and Growth in Mature Economics: The Case of Belgium (New York: Macmillan, 1961), p. 28.

1970 figures: calculated by the author from L'Economie Belge en 1970 (Brussels: Belgian Ministry of Economic Affairs), pp. 358-59.

percent in 1958 to 68.5 percent in 1970.[14] This figure probably understates the trade creation effect. Belgium's exports to the Netherlands, which had the lowest nominal tariffs before the Treaty of Rome, and hence where the trade creation effect is the smallest, have remained remarkably steady over the 1958-67 period. Belgium's exports to the Netherlands as a percentage of total exports was 20.7 in 1958 and 19.4 in 1970. The other three EEC countries, all with considerably higher external tariffs prior to the formation of the Common Market and with much greater domestic markets, have all taken much larger shares of Belgian exports. West Germany took 24.6 percent of total Belgian exports in 1970 (1958 = 11.6 percent), France had 19.8 percent (1958 = 10.6 percent) and Italy imported 4.7 percent (1958 = 2.3 percent). The total for these three major EEC partners was 49.2 percent in 1970 compared to 24.5 percent in 1958, an increase of 98 percent in the value of Belgian exports to Italy, France, and West Germany since the EEC has been in existence.

BELGIAN REGIONAL STRUCTURE

The regions that will be utilized for the purposes of this study are the nine political provinces of Belgium. Occasionally reference

will be made of the smaller political subdivisions of the provinces—
the districts—of which there are forty-four. This will be the case in
discussing particular cities such as Brussels and Antwerp, which are
districts as well as cities. The focus on political regions as opposed
to various types of economic functional regions is necessitated by the
data base.

The nine provinces are Antwerp, Limburg, East Flanders, West
Flanders, Brabant, Liege, Namur, Hainaut, and Luxembourg. Antwerp,
Limburg, and East and West Flanders are Flemish-speaking provinces;
Liege, Namur, Hainaut, and Luxembourg are French-speaking provinces. Brabant contains Brussels, which is French-speaking, the
southern district of Nivelles, which is also French-speaking, and the
two Flemish-speaking districts of Halle-Vilvoorde and Louvain. The
total French-speaking area, not including Brussels, is called "Wallonie,"
while the remaining four provinces are Flemish-speaking.

The total Flemish population of Belgium in 1969 was 5,404,000
(56 percent of the total), the Wallonie population was 3,122,000 (32
percent of the total) and the citizens of Brussels and its periphery
numbered 1,073,000 (11 percent of the total). [15]

Table 6 is a compilation of population figures, working population
as a percentage of total population, employment as a percentage of
working population, unemployment rates, and per capita GDP (gross
domestic product) at factor cost. From this table there are several
facts of immediate interest concerning Belgian regional structure.
The first is that, in general, the Flemish provinces have a slightly
higher working population than do the French, with the exception of
Limburg, which is the poorest province in Belgium. Conversely,
Brussels, which accounts for the preponderant amount of the population
and GDP figure for the province of Brabant, has the highest rate of
working population and the highest per capita GDP. The second observation is that the figure for actual employment in the province as
a percentage of total people resident in the province or district available to work varies to an extreme degree. In the city of Brussels
there are 43 percent more people working than there are workers
residing. In the opposite cases, in both Limburg and Luxembourg,
only 80 percent of the resident workers are able to find jobs in their
own region. Hence a low employment as a percentage of the working
population figure can hide two contradictory trends. A low percentage
figure in column 4 can mean that a large part of the resident working
population of the province works in another province where the demand for employment is greater. Alternatively, it can mean large
unemployment in the province.

The unemployment rate, when considered with employment as a
percentage of working population, provides information with which
employment in and migration from the provinces can be better

TABLE 6

Selected Regional Statistics

(1) Province	(2) Population (1969) (thousands)	(3) Available Working Population as percent of Total Population (1967)	(4) Employment in Province as a percent of Working Force of Province (1967)	(5) Unemployment Rate	(6) Per Capita GPP at Factor Cost, Current Prices in U.S. dollars
Antwerp	1,531	37.8	99.5	2.0	1,811
West Flanders	1,052	37.9	91.0	2.1	1,558
East Flanders	1,311	39.2	83.0	2.2	1,356
Limburg	651	33.4	80.0	3.5	1,235
Hainaut	1,331	33.0	91.7	3.5	1,418
Liege	1,016	37.0	98.2	4.1	1,782
Luxembourg	219	36.9	80.0	1.6	1,280
Namur	383	35.2	85.5	1.6	1,510
Brabant	2,166				
Flemish districts	792	38.1	76.0	.9 ⎫	⎫
French districts	229	34.4	87.2	1.6 ⎬	2,090
Brussels	1,145	42.4	143.0	1.8 ⎭	⎭
Total Belgium	9,660	37.5	96.8	2.4	1,650

Source: Column 2 is from Institution National de Statistique, Annuaire Statistique de la Belgique 1970, pp. 38–39. Columns 3 and 4 are from Ministry of Economic Affairs. Column 5 was calculated by the author by dividing the people claiming or receiving unemployment for each region in 1967 by the total working population of that region. The numerator was from Institut National de Statistique, Bulletin de Statistique, No. 4-S (April-May, 1969), p. 466. The denominator was the absolute figure represented in Column 3.
Column 6 was obtained by dividing the provincial GPP at factor cost by the 1967 populations of the provinces.

13

evaluated. When the unemployment rate is high and the employment
as a percentage of working population figure is low, then it is safe
to assume that the primary reason for the lowness of this second
figure is due to large unemployment. This is the case for the provinces
of Limburg and Hainaut. When the unemployment figure is low and
the percentage of employment of working population is also low, then
this would indicate large numbers of migrant workers. This is the
case in Flemish- and French-speaking districts near Brussels and
for the parts of East Flanders contingent to Antwerp.

The most puzzling statistics are those for Luxembourg and
Namur. In both provinces there is a low unemployment rate and a low
employment as a percent of working population rate, which is normal
for regions that have large numbers of commuters to other provinces.
But the locations of Namur and particularly of Luxembourg are not
advantageous for communting to the high-growth centers of Antwerp
and Brussels. This discrepancy is partially explained by the fact
that Luxembourg and Namur are the two provinces most heavily
oriented toward agriculture, which contributed 22 percent and 12.5
percent of the provincial GPP, (gross provincial product)in 1967
for Luxembourg and Namur, respectively, as compared to a national
average of 5.8 percent. Given the lack of industry in these provinces
and the importance of agriculture, many workers are not engaged in
industrial work, which accounts for the low employment as a percentage
of working population figure. A comparatively large number of workers
are engaged in small agricultural activities and hence are not eligible
for unemployment protection (accounting for the low rate of unemployment).

The GPP per capita at factor cost figures by province also
revealed striking differences in regional income in 1966.[16] These
range from a low of $1,235 for the province of Limburg to a high of
$2,090 for the province of Brabant. The average per capita GPP at
factor cost for Belgium was $1,650 in 1966.* The mean per capita
GDP at factor cost was $1,560, reflecting the relatively heavier
weights of the richer provinces that make the average for the country
greater than the mean for the provinces. The levels of Belgian provincial income are highly unequal and, in fact, so disbursed as to be

---

*The provincial GDP at factor cost was selected in this example
for two reasons. First, provincial figures on GDP are not available
at this time. Second, and more important, when discussing differences
in regional income so as to evaluate a government regional development program, it is preferable to discuss real regional differences
and hence to remove from the discussion the effects of subsidies and
taxes. This is accomplished by the use of the factor cost concept.

statistically improbable as tested against a small sample statistical distribution.[17]

One of the best systematic works of the regional development problems of Belgium was made by L. H. Klaassen.[18] In this study, using 1959 data, he divides the eight provinces and the districts of the cities of Brussels, Louvain, and Nivelles into four groups. The criteria for group selection was (1) the position of the province or district relative to the national average in per capita GPP, and (2) the rate of increase of provincial or district GPP relative to the national average. These two categories were then placed in a matrix, which is reproduced as Table 7.

From this matrix Klaassen concludes that there are four categories of regions in Belgium:

1. High prosperity regions such as Antwerp and Brussels.
2. Depressed regions that are in the process of development including the provinces of West Flanders, East Flanders, Namur, and the neighboring districts to Brussels of Nivelles and Louvain.
3. Potential depressed areas such as Liege.
4. Depressed areas such as Limburg, Luxembourg, and Hainaut.[19]

If it is assumed that the rate of change in GPP is proportional to the level of employment in the province and Klaassen's method is applied to the data in Table 6 the results are almost identical.

TABLE 7

Classification of Belgian Regions

Rate of Increase	Level of Income	
	High	Low
High	Antwerp Brussels	West Flanders East Flanders Louvain Nivelles Namur
Low	Liege	Luxembourg Hainaut Limburg

Source: L. H. Klaassen, Area Economic and Social Development (Paris: Organization for Economic Cooperation and Development, 1965), p. 31.

Antwerp and Brabant which includes Brussels, (unfortunately there
was no district breakdown for Nivelles and Louvain, in 1966) were
the only two provinces with greater than national average per capita
GPP in 1966 that also had a lower than Belgian average unemployment
rate. The Brabant and Antwerp per capita GPPs were $2,090 and
$1,811, respectively, as compared to Belgium's figure of $1,650, while
unemployment was .9 percent and 2.0 percent, respectively, compared
to the national average of 2.4 percent. These would be prosperity
regions. Liege was the only province with a greater per capita GPP
($1,782) that also had a higher than national average unemployment
rate (4.1 percent), making it a potentially depressed region. The
provinces of West Flanders, East Flanders, and Namur were all
under national averages for both per capita GPP and unemployment
($1,356 and $1,510, respectively, for East Flander's and Namur's per
capita income, while the unemployment rates were 2.2 percent and
1.6 percent), indicating provinces in the process of development.
The provinces of Hainaut and Limburg had lower GPP's than the
average for Belgium combined with higher than national average unemployment rates (Limburg had $1,235 GPP per capita with 3.5 percent
unemployment, while Hainaut recorded a $1,418 income and 3.5 percent
unemployment), placing these two in the depressed province category.
The only exception to Klaassen's classification is with province of
Luxembourg, which has one of the lowest GPPs in Belgium, but because
it is by far the most agricultural province the unemployment rate is
low.* Because of its exceptionally low per capita income (the second
lowest among the provinces in 1966) Luxembourg must be considered
as a depressed province.**

The conclusion to this brief study of Belgian industrial and
regional structure is that while the industrial structure changed a
great deal in the period from 1958 to 1967, the regional structure
over approximately the same time remained remarkably unchanged.
The advances in industrial output, the increased allocation of investment to more profitable and productive sectors, and the great advance
in national income per capita were not accompanied by a trend toward
regional income equalization. As has been seen, the same analysis
of regional development, using 1959 data, can be equally applied to
1966 data; and, with only one exception, the groupings of the provinces
into four stages of regional development were identical.

In addition, according to 1966 data, there still existed an extreme
dispersion of income per capita on the provincial level. The province
of lowest per capita GPP at factor cost (Limburg) was 25 percent

---

*Twenty-two of the GPP of Luxembourg is provided by agricul-
ture against the national average of 5.8 percent.
**See Table 13, p. 41.

below the national average and almost 42 percent below that of the highest provincial GPP (Brabant).* The distribution of income among the provinces was so skewed that the probability of finding a provincial income per capita as high as that of Brabant is less than 1 in 1,000 and the probability of finding an income as low as Limburg's is less than 1 in 100.20 The fact that there was no tendency toward regional income equalization, even during a decade of unprecedented economic growth at the national level, provided the incentive to revise and enlarge the framework of the regional development effort.

---

*Calculated from the figures given in column 6 of Table 6.

CHAPTER

2

**THE INVESTMENT
INCENTIVE
PROGRAM**

INTRODUCTION

This chapter discusses the administrative response to the changes
in the Belgian economy covered in Chapter 1. Its first section considers the legal framework of Belgian investment incentive policy.
It is designed to provide the factual basis concerning the relation
between regional and national investment incentives, the criteria for
the selection of depressed regions, the various categories of aid, and
the types of incentives offered by the Belgian government. The second
section is a qualitative discussion of the trends in the interpretation
of the regional development laws. It will examine the types of incentives the government has believed to be the most successful, changing
market conditions and their effect upon the incentive program, and the
trend toward project analysis in the administration of incentives.

THE LEGAL FRAMEWORK OF THE
INVESTMENT INCENTIVE PROGRAM

The legal framework of the investment incentive program is
provided by three laws. These are the laws of July 17, 1959, July 18,
1959, and July 14, 1966. The Law of July 17, 1959 is general in nature
and applies to all of Belgium. The laws of July 18, 1959 and July 14,
1966 are uniquely concerned with regional development. The three
laws are intended to be considered as a "single legislative program
whose purpose is to promote economic expansion by encouraging
industrial investments."[1] In fact, as will be documented later in this
chapter and in Chapter 3, the Law of July 14, 1966 was a new attempt

to stimulate regional development following the failure of the Law of July 18, 1959 to accomplish this task.*

The laws of July 17 and 18, 1959 were designed to strengthen the Belgian economic and regional structure before the full effect of Belgium's entrance into the Common Market was felt. The major weaknesses in the Belgian economy in 1959 were high unemployment, low profit margins (with a concomitant low investment rate) lack of a modern industrial base producing high demand products, and uneven regional development.** The aims of the Law of July 17, 1959 were intended to resolve or alleviate all of these problems. The aims of the law were "the creation of jobs in the general framework of the Government's employment policy, the creation of new industries and the manufacture of new products, the expansion of existing firms in their adaption to new market conditions, improvement in the position of depressed economic sectors, the improvement in labor conditions or in the operating conditions of the firm by increased productivity or profitability, and the expansion of research."[2]

The Law of July 18, 1959 was uniquely concerned with regional development. This law calls for aid in certain regions "faced with economic and social problems."[3] The exact criteria for the designation of these development areas are those regions that have one or more of the following characteristics:

1. Permanent unemployment.
2. Development endangered by the large migration of inhabitants to other regions.
3. Seasonal, weekly, or daily commuting of a large number of inhabitants.
4. The impending or real decline of important economic activities to the region.[4]

The four main interests of the Belgian government in 1959 as summarized from the objectives of the laws of July 17 and 18 are the maintenance of an adequate level of domestic employment, the importation of new technological methods, the modernization of industrial structure, and the promotion of regional development. These are still the principal concerns of Belgian economic decisionmakers, although the priorities have perhaps been changed because of the relative achievement of the first three objectives and the lack of success of the fourth until the late 1960s.***

---

*This will be discussed further in Chapter 3.

**See Chapter 1, section called "Belgian Industrial Structure."

***In addition to the published aims of the government, these same priorities were expressed to the author during meetings with officials

The Law of July 14, 1966 provided for aid that could be granted "in order to promote and accelerate the reconversion and economic development of the coal mining regions and certain other regions confronted with critical or urgent problems."[5] The aid may be given to projects that "contribute to the rapid creation of industrial activities."[6] This is further defined as a type of project that would tend to diversify the economic activity of the region, favor the installation of rapid growth or high value-added industries, provide work for available manpower, and promote scientific research.[7]

There are four categories of aid and each category is entitled to a different amount of incentives. The Law of July 17, 1959 has the two categories of General Aid and Special Aid. In theory both of these categories are applicable to all of Belgium. General Aid is given for those projects that give promise of fulfilling the list of national economic objectives that were discussed earlier. Special Aid is a higher incentive category for projects that are subject to two constraints: (1) the investment project must "require a financial outlay materially in excess of what the firm might normally provide for new capital formation";[8] (2) the project must have a stimulating effect on economic activity, within the objectives of government planning, that is clear beyond all doubt.[9]

The Law of July 18, 1959 provides for Regional Aid for those projects undertaken in the specified development areas. The development areas were delimited by the selective use of one or more of the four characteristics of depressed areas. The largest areas delimited as development areas were in the provinces of Luxembourg, Hainaut, and West Flanders. A large development area was also delimited around the point where the three provinces of Antwerp, Brabant, and Limburg have a common border. The total population resident in the development areas was 15 percent of the Belgian total in 1959.[10]

The Law of July 14, 1966 increased both the amount of subsidy available for development areas and the extent of these areas. The category of aid that increased the incentives was Exceptional Aid, and it was specifically designed to assist in the conversion of the coal mining regions to other types of industry. The development areas previously delimited by the Regional Law of 1959 were almost all included in the expanded areas under the Law of 1966, the exception being the largely agricultural region of Luxembourg. In addition, the development areas were extended to cover most of Limburg, much of West Flanders, the southern part of East Flanders, central Liege (around the City of Liege), and western Hainaut to Charleroi. The

---

in the Ministry of Economic Affairs (March, 1968) and the Belgian Consulate in New York City. (November-December, 1969.)

development areas of Belgium for the 1959 and 1966 regional laws
are shown in Figure 2.

The Belgian government offers incentives for three categories
of investments. These are investment in fixed assets, intangible
assets (organizational studies, research and development, and new
product development), and other basic costs relating to the marketing
of a new product that has been created by the operations of an eligible
investment.

There are five types of financial assistance presently given by
the Belgian government to eligible investments:[11] (1) interest rate
subsidies, (2) direct capital grants, (3) state guarantees, (4) tax
advantages, and (5) interest-free advances.* A project may receive
one or more of the five incentives. Each type of incentive is linked
to a certain category of aid, so that investments operating under the
Exceptional Aid provisions of the Law of 1966 would receive a considerably larger subsidy than another investment classified under the
General Aid category of the Law of July 17, 1958.

The interest rate subsidy is the most important form of investment incentive offered by the Belgian government. It is paid directly
to approved credit organizations, who in turn loan the agreed amount
to the project management at the market rate of interest minus the
rate of subsidy paid by the government.[12] The interest subsidy will
apply to an amount equal to one half or two thirds of the value of the
fixed assets of the investment, the higher figure being granted for
those projects in regional development areas of the 1966 laws. In
the case of General Aid, Special Aid, or Regional Aid, the length of
the interest rate subsidy is normally between three and five years.
In cases of Exceptional Aid, the length of the subsidy period is five
years.[13]

The interest rate subsidy is a maximum of two percentage points
per annum in the case of General Aid, and four percentage points per
annum maximum for Special and Regional Aid, subject to the constraint that the effective interest rate paid by the recipient of the
subsidy is greater than one percent. In the case of Exceptional Aid
the interest subsidy may be as high as five percentage points per
annum and, in special cases of a highly desirable investment in a
1966 development area, may cover the entire interest expense of the
project (up to the amount of two thirds of fixed assets) for the first
two years, and then five percentage points for the next three years.
The interest rates charged on term loans by the Societe Nationale de

---

*The preeminence of the interest rate subsidy has been related
to the author by Belgian officials and American bankers and business-
men.

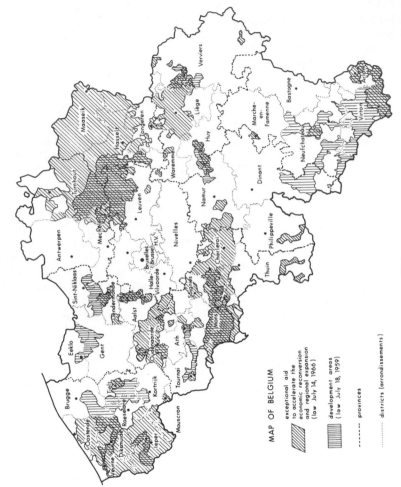

MAP OF BELGIUM

exceptional aid
to accelerate the
economic reconversion
and regional expansion
(law July 14, 1966)

development areas
(law July 18, 1959)

------ provinces

.... districts (arrondissements)

Source: Belgian Ministry of Economic Affairs.

Credit à l'Industrie (SNCI) are market rates. The increase in the
long-term interest rate has increased the relative attractiveness
of having a desirable project in an Exceptional Aid area. The rate
of interest at the SNCI went from 6.75 percent per annum for a term
loan of up to five years and 7.0 percent for more than five years in
May, 1966 to the rates of 8.75 percent for up to five years and 9.00
percent for more than five years in late 1969.[14] This means that
the 1969 subsidy differential between such a project and a project
benefiting from the maximum amount of General Aid was 6.75 percent
per annum (8.75 percent-2 percent) for the first two years of the
amount subsidized.[15] The interest rate subsidy amount may not be
taken in the form of a lump sum payment.

Direct capital grants may also be made under the Law of July
14, 1966. The amount of the grant is limited to the amount of the
interest subsidy that would have been provided had the investor desired
interest expense benefits as opposed to direct capital grants. The
capital grant and the interest subsidy, either separately or combined,
are calculated on a base that may not exceed two thirds of the investment in fixed assets.[16] For example, an investment in fixed assets
of BF (Belgian francs) 150 million in an exceptional aid area would
have a base eligible for subsidy of BF 100 million (2/3 x BF 150
million).

It is possible to obtain the full amount of the capital grant at
the time a favorable decision is made by the government concerning
the granting of incentives to the project. This is opposed to the
procedure with the interest rate subsidy of receiving the amount of
subsidy over the period when the interest expense is due. Here the
direct capital grant as a lump-sum payment has advantages to the
investor over the interest rate subsidy, which is an annuity, for time
value of money reasons. In practice, foreign firms take the interest
rate subsidy when they need to borrow Belgian capital and take the
direct capital grant when they do not need local capital.[17] Because
there are several factors at the present time that make local borrowing more attractive, foreign firms tend to take the interest rate
subsidy and borrow the money locally.[18] It is important to note,
however, that it is possible to take the capital grant and also borrow
money locally at the market rate of interest. This combination of
actions, which most firms have overlooked, could result in substantial
profit gains derived from the tax-deductible nature of interest expense
in Belgium and the time value of money advantage conferred by the
lump-sum payment of the capital grant.[19]

The State Guarantee is granted to the credit institutions loaning
money to the recipient of this incentive. It guarantees the total or
partial reimbursement of interest, principal, and other charges
related to the credit institution giving the loan. It is granted in

instances where the private guarantee of the investor is not considered
adequate by the credit institution relative to the size of the loan. The
guarantee may be total if the loan is given by a semipublic credit
institution (the SNCI for example) and up to 50 percent of the uncovered
amount of the loan if it has been granted by a private institution.
For projects benefiting from incentives under the Law of July 14, 1966
the percentage of the uncovered amount guaranteed by the state was
raised to 75 percent.[20]

The fourth primary type of incentive consists of various tax
advantages. These do not have the importance of the other incentives
to foreign investors because they are generally very small in amount
and/or short in duration. The various tax credits offered by Belgium
are an exemption on real property, income tax, exemption from
taxation of the direct capital grant, reduction of capital gains tax upon
reinvestment in Belgium, and exemption from the Capital Registration
Tax of 1.5 percent of invested capital. These exemptions are almost
limited to those projects qualifying for incentives of the 1966 Law.
The only exemption allowed under the earlier laws was the real
property income tax exemption, which in 1966 was raised to maximum
of ten years.[21]

An additional exemption given only under the 1966 Law is the
use of accelerated depreciation within specified limits for specified
types of assets. Companies benefiting from this incentive may now
charge their depreciation on a double declining balance method for
the first three years. This is not as great an advantage as in the
United States, because Belgian tax law makes the published financial
statements the basis for tax payments. This eliminates the use of
straight-line depreciation for published public statements (which
shows a greater profit) and the simultaneous use of accelerated
depreciation for tax purposes (showing lower profit and lower tax
liability), which can be done in the United States.[22]

The fifth and last form of incentive offered by the Belgian
government is interest-free advances for research and development
reasons. These loans may not exceed 80 percent of the amount
actually spent by the investor. The advances are to be used to develop
"prototypes, new products, or manufacturing processes to be used
in Belgium."[23]

In conclusion, there are two primary points of importance: first,
Belgian economic priorities were changed in this period and second,
the basic methods of dealing with the problems were not. The change
in priorities between 1959 and 1966 is evidenced by the fact that the
first consideration of the Belgian government in 1959 was to primary
problems of industrial structure and unemployment. As has been
seen from the study of industrial structure at that time, this was a
warranted calculation of priorities. The role of regional development

became more important as Belgium's macroeconomic problems were alleviated and culminated with the Law of July 14, 1966, which raised the priority of the depressed areas program.

The 1966 Law, although widened geographically and deepened in terms of increased incentives, did not offer a fundamentally new approach to dealing with the problems of regional development areas.

TRENDS IN THE APPLICATION OF REGIONAL DEVELOPMENT INVESTMENT INCENTIVES

The most important trend in the administration of the regional development program has been the increasing emphasis on project analysis as condition for government aid.[24] The simple act of choosing a depressed area as the site for a plant does not automatically guarantee a foreign investor with the highest possible incentives under the Exceptional Aid program. Exceptional Aid is reserved for a highly desirable investment in terms of employment and technology for an industry that decides to locate in a depressed area. Despite this increasing trend toward project analysis, it is fair to state that, on the average, the firms locating in the officially delimited development areas of the Law of July 14, 1966 have benefited from relatively fixed-rate higher incentives than those that did not. Similarly, it is fair to assume that those firms locating in the immediate area of Antwerp or Brussels during the past two years have received on the average smaller incentives than those locating elsewhere in nondesignated developed areas. The relatively greater prosperity of the Antwerp and Brussels areas has meant that the government is reluctant to subsidize any investment in these two areas.

The most important incentive among the five types offered by the Belgian government has proved to be the interest rate subsidy. The increase in Belgian interest rates during 1967-69 added to the amount of subsidy given a desirable project under Exceptional Aid, because in the first two years of the project the entire interest expense is paid by the government. The following three cases illustrate the workings of the interest rate subsidy with regard to maximum incentives for an investment in a 1966 regional development area, an average investment in a 1966 regional development area, and an investment not in a regional development area that benefits from General Aid.[25] (See also Table 8.)

Case I: An investment of maximum incentive in a development area of the 1966 Law. This assumes an investment of BF 150 million in fixed assets, a ten-year term load for BF 100, million (two thirds of BF 150 million) repayable in ten annual installments, and an interest rate of nine percent.

TABLE 8

Three Subsidy Cases for Investment in Fixed
Assets of BF 150 Million

	Year	Loan Out-standing (BF millions)	Interest Subsidy Granted (percent)	Incentive Received (BF millions)	Total Incentive as Percent of Total Fixed Assets
Case I	1	100	9.0	9.0	
	2	90	9.0	8.1	
	3	80	5.0	4.0	
	4	70	5.0	3.5	
	5	60	5.0	3.0	
			Total incentive:	27.6	18.2 (= 27.1/150)
Case II	1	100	5.0	5.0	
	2	90	5.0	4.5	
	3	80	5.0	4.0	
	4	70	5.0	3.5	
	5	60	5.0	3.0	
			Total incentive:	20.0	13.3 (= 20.0/150)
Case III	1	75	2.0	1.5	
	2	67.5	2.0	1.4	
	3	60	2.0	1.2	
	4	52.5	2.0	1.1	
	5	45	2.0	.9	
			Total incentive:	6.1	4.1 (= 6.1/150)

Source: Modified from Ministry of Economic Affairs, "Summary of Incentives to Foreign Investment," (Brussels, 1968), p. 4.

Case II: All monetary details are the same except the investment is being made by a company of only average attractiveness to the Belgian government, as opposed to the exceptionally attractive investments considered in Case I.

Case III: All details are the same except the investment is not located in a development area, but it benefits from General Aid (Law of July 17, 1959) which drops the base upon which the subsidy is calculated from two thirds to one half of fixed assets.

It should be remembered that these cases are only theoretical and that in fact the actual incentive is the result of negotiation, which often results in a relatively uniform subsidy.

In addition to the cheapness of Belgian loans, as compared with the Eurodollar market (even without the subsidy), another point of importance has been the availability of domestic money. It is particularly important to American firms that, since January 1, 1968, have not been free to export capital from the United States. In addition to plentiful debt instruments, the Belgian government offers the use of SNI (Societe National d'Investissement) to take 90 percent of the equity participation of a foreign firm and leave the management control of the firm with the foreign entity. This measure was taken after the Office of Foreign Direct Investments, Department of Commerce controls were initiated in 1968 because investments in firms that were owned less than 10 percent by the American investor were exempted from these controls.[26]

In conclusion to this section, the Belgian government has been very aware of internal and external money conditions and has acted very quickly to prevent any harmful effects from these affecting the regional development program. Although there has been an increased trend toward project analysis most incentives are probably decided by giving automatically "x" size incentives for any firm locating in a regional development region. The division of the country into only two zones probably accounts partially for the limited flexibility of the regional program.

This review on the legal framework of investment incentives as the government's response to economic conditions in the country can not be studied in a vacuum. To complete the picture the reaction of foreign investors to the incentive program must also be considered. This will be discussed in Chapter 3.

3

FOREIGN INVESTMENT
AND THE REGIONAL
INVESTMENT INCENTIVE
PROGRAM

INTRODUCTION

This chapter deals with the reactions of foreign investors to the investment incentive program discussed in Chapter 2. It evaluates the effectiveness of the program, given the aims of the government. It will discuss the following results of the incentive program:

1. The success of the incentives in attracting foreign investment to regional development areas.
2. The economic characteristics of the industries that have higher propensity to invest in the development areas.
3. An assessment of the importance of these characteristics to the regional development of the depressed areas.
4. Implications of the regional incentive program for national and regional distribution of investment.

The chapter has three sections. The first is a study of the background of foreign investment in Belgium and a brief discussion of the sectorial and regional distribution of the incentives over the 1959-68 period.

The second section considers the characteristics of the firms investing in the depressed regions. There is little discussion of the individual firms; discussion centers instead on the types of industries that are attracted to these areas. The first characteristics studied are the distribution of foreign firms in Belgium in 1968 and 1969 (the first two full years after the enactment of the 1966 Law) by nationality (American and other foreign), by size of investment, and by industry. The industries are broken down by their propensity to invest in development areas, and each industry is analyzed in relation to productivity, profits, exports, demand for product, labor intensity, and other economic characteristics desired by the Belgian government.

The third section is a study of the implications of plant location and industrial characteristics as revealed the section on regional development. These include the distribution effects of the investment incentives, exogenous economic policies that could negatively affect the incentive program, possible tariff effects on the incentive program, and finally, the welfare and the real growth effects of the type of investment attracted to the depressed areas.

FOREIGN FIRMS: THEIR DECISION TO INVEST IN BELGIUM, THE SIZE OF NEW FOREIGN INVESTMENT, AND THE AMOUNT OF INCENTIVES GIVEN

The creation of the Common Market was the primary factor that induced the great increase in foreign investment in Belgium from 1958 to the present.[1] The theory is that trade and investment are substitutes so that the artificial limitation of one by tariffs acts to increase the size of the other. The trade diversion effects of increased protection are accompanied by a similar investment creation effect. Moreover, the strength of the investment creation effect is directly proportional to the strength of the trade diversion effect. Because the trade diversion effect of the EEC was very large owing to the market size of the partners, similarly the investment creation effect was very strong. Other empirical studies, including the author's, focus upon market size and other variables as being determining factors.[2]

This argument has to be modified for the specific case of Belgium and must take into account the gradual nature of the tariff changes. The Treaty of Rome specified that internal tariffs among members of the EEC would be progressively lowered.[3] The common exterior duty would be an unweighted average of the tariffs of the four partner groups. This meant a lower final exterior tariff for France and Italy, a slightly higher final exterior tariff for West Germany, and considerably higher tariff for the Benelux countries.[4]

The progressive nature of these tariff changes over time on an intra-Common Market basis implied that the full strength of the investment creation effect would not benefit the Benelux countries until the internal duties were nearly or completely eliminated and the exterior tariff was raised to its full height. Consider the position of a prospective American investor as the market existed in 1960. The choice of Belgium as a location for his investment was not a rational one as regards tariffs.[5] First, if he is interested primarily in the Benelux domestic market, he may export from the United States and take advantage of the still low exterior tariffs on the Benelux countries. Second, if he were interested in locating in Belgium and exporting

to the other EEC countries, he would be better off to locate in Italy,
France, or Germany, produce for their large domestic markets with
no tariff, and export to the low-tariff Benelux countries. By locating
in the Benelux countries a foreign investor has the disadvantage of a
smaller domestic market and, in 1960, still would face high tariffs
from the other EEC countries. The result is that foreign (mainly
American) investment in Belgium tended to lag behind the rates of
increase of American investment elsewhere in the EEC for the late
1950s and the early 1960s. This point is illustrated by the calculation
of the index of increase in book value of American investments in the
EEC. The Belgian average did not pass the EEC average until 1966
and in the early 1960s lagged seriously behind it at approximately
two thirds of the Common Market rate. But Belgium's rate of increase
in book value of American investment began to increase relative to
that of the Common Market in 1963. In 1970 the Belgian index of book
value of American investment was 968, while the Common Market
average was 752 (1957 = 100).[6]
     The second point concerns relative amounts of new American
and other foreign investment. American investment has amounted to
well over 70 percent of total new foreign investment in the period
1959-67, before dropping to just over 29.5 percent in 1968-70, partially
as a result of the OFDI restrictions.[7] A graph of total new foreign
investment and its American component is shown in Figure 3.
     The amount of incentive paid by the Belgian government is
unfortunately not broken down by the laws under which it is given.
However, a study of the increases in investments benefiting from
incentive payments in 1967 and 1968 relative to the size of the investment flow can give us an idea of the increase caused by the 1966 Law.
Figure 3 illustrates the flow of new foreign investment into Belgium
in the period 1959-70. The amounts have varied considerably from
year to year, but the two-year average for 1967-68 of BF 11.4 billion
is only 5.6 percent over the 1964-66 average of BF 10.8 billion annually. This set of figures may be compared with the amount of investment that benefited from incentives in the same period for all of
Belgium. The amount of total investment that benefited from incentives
in the 1964-66 period was an annual average of BF 20.2 billion (that
was 14.7 percent of gross capital formation excluding housing for
this period).[8] In 1967-68, this had increased to BF 35.2 billion, which
amounted to 22 percent of the gross capital formation excluding
housing for this period. As has been shown, this was not the result
of large new foreign investment or of a substantial increase in domestic capital formation (see Table 1). It was the effect of the 1966 Law
that made a larger proportion of Belgian investment eligible for
incentive aid.[9] The total investment that received incentives in 1967
and 1968 accounted for 34 percent of the total amount of incentives

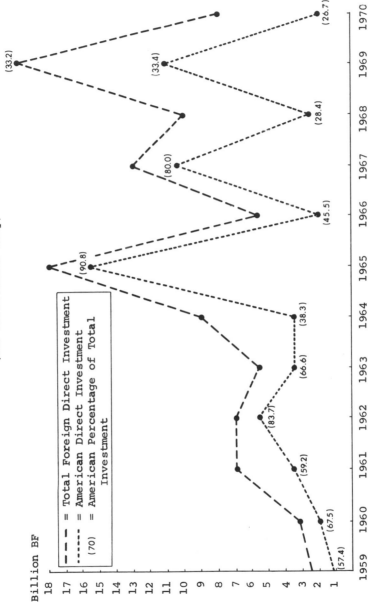

FIGURE 3

American and All Foreign Direct Investment in Belgium, 1959-70
(new investments only)

Billion BF

- - - = Total Foreign Direct Investment
.... = American Direct Investment
(70) = American Percentage of Total
        Investment

Sources: Belgian Ministry of Economic Affairs, L'Investissement Etrangers
en Belgique (Brussels, 1966, 1967, 1968, 1969, and 1970).

31

given between 1959 and 1968, despite the fact that these two years comprised only 20 percent of the time period in which incentives had been offered.10

The amount of new foreign investment as a percentage of total investment eligible for incentives between 1959 and 1968 was 33.6 percent. The preponderance of this new foreign investment took place in the sectors of metals, metallic fabrications, and chemicals. In these industries the foreign percentage of total new investment eligible for incentives was 32.5 percent, 52.8 percent and 37.5 percent, respectively.11

The political implications of new foreign plant location can be seen by Table 9. Despite higher unemployment rates and lower

TABLE 9

Provinces Benefiting from Incentives in the Years 1959-70*

1	2	3
Province or District	Amount of Foreign or Joint Belgian- Foreign New Investment Benefiting from Incentives (BF millions)	Column 2 as Percent of Total Investment Benefiting From Incentives**
1. Antwerp	25.3	33.5
2. West Flanders	1.4	7.3
3. East Flanders	26.3	43.0
4. Limburg	16.9	50.6
5. Flemish Brabant	1.9	20.7
Flemish totals	71.8	36.9
6. Hainaut	19.9	32.2
7. Liege	4.4	9.1
8. Luxembourg	.8	21.6
9. Namur	.1	1.4
10. Walloon Brabant (district)	.4	3.2
French totals	25.6	13.5
11. Brussels City		.1
Belgian totals	97.4	28.7

*Incentives from the laws of July 17 and 18, 1959 and July 14, 1966.
**Includes new and existing investments.

Source: Calculated by author from L'Investissement Etrangers en Belgique (Brussels, 1970 report), Table 9, p. xiv.

growth rates in Wallonie area, 59 percent of the incentive-sponsored investment has been made in Flemish regions as opposed to only 39.4 percent in French regions. The Belgian new investment and additions to old investment that fall under the incentives laws are only slightly lower in the French provinces (BF 107.9 billion between 1959-70 in the French provinces as opposed to BF 126.5 billion in the Flemish). The preference of new foreign investors for the Flemish provinces (73.2 percent of new foreign investment locating in Belgium in 1959-70) means that the total subsidized investment in Belgium was going primarily into the Flemish area.12 Before a study of the broad implications of the incentive program can be attempted, the effects of the 1966 Law must be considered in detail.

THE EFFECTS OF THE 1966 LAW ON
FOREIGN INVESTMENT

As has been illustrated, the 1966 Law increased both maximum rate of the subsidy given to foreign firms and the geographic regions over which these subsidies were payable. The changes in both factors acted to augment incentive payments. The purpose of this section is to investigate the specific economic characteristics of the foreign industries locating new plants in Belgium between 1967-70.13*

The total number of new industrial investments during 1967-70 was 273.13 The actual number of new plant locations was 124 because two investments involved two new plant locations each. While this number is only 11 percent of the total number of new foreign ventures in Belgium between 1967 and 1970, it accounts for 89 percent of the total value of investment for these two years.14 This disparity is explained by the large number of sales offices, small service organizations, and other foreign affiliates that count as new foreign investment but have an inconsequential capital base. These small units were omitted from this study because of their size. In addition, several of the headquarters of the firms considered in this study were located in Brussels, while the plants were located elsewhere. In this situation only the plant location was considered because of its greater economic consequences for regional development.

Of the total 273 industrial investments between 1967 and 1970, 180 were located in regional development areas set up under the 1966

---

*These years were selected because they are the first year after the passage of the 1966 Law and the last year on which data are available.

Law.[15] The total propensity to invest in underdeveloped regions was
66 percent (180/273).

By nationality 106 of the 273 new industrial investments (39
percent) were American or joint American-Belgian ventures.[16] The
remaining 167 plants were constructed by other foreign or other
foreign with minority Belgian partnership. This figure represents
61 percent of the total new foreign plants.[17] The new American
investment is proportionately large relative to its share in the areas
around the cities of Liege and Charleroi. The "other foreign" plant
location is proportionately large relative to its share in East Antwerp
and the province of Limburg (where it is the only foreign investment).
In addition, the "other foreign" investment provides more urban
concentration than does the American, with five or more new plant
locations in the cities of Brussels and Liege. In relation to propensity
to invest in the 1966 depressed areas, the "other foreign" investment
had 110 of its total 167 new plant locations in these depressed areas
(65.8 percent). For new American plant locations, the figures were
70 of the total 106, giving a propensity to invest in development
regions (PIDR) of 66.0 percent.[18] Despite a smaller number of new
plant locations, the Americans nevertheless invested more, which
implies larger investment projects.[19] As will be shown below, the
propensity to invest in regional development areas declines with the
size of the investment.

New foreign investment was also subdivided into three categories
by size. The size of an investment is measured by its capitalization.
The U.S. dollar equivalent of the categories are first,those investments less than BF 10 million; second, BF 10-49.9 million; and
finally, those greater than BF 50 million. First, the investment by
size data are 83 percent of the total (227/273 = 82 percent). Second,
the propensity to invest in depressed areas is 68 percent (154 out of
227), which is almost the same as that of the entire sample (180/273
= 66 percent).[20]

The PIDR declines by category as the size of the investment
becomes larger. For the grouping of new plant locations in the BF 0
to 10 million category, 80 of the total 112 new sites (71 percent) were
in regional development areas. For the medium firms (capitalization
of BF 10-49.9 million), the percentage investing in depressed areas
dropped to 67 percent (45 of 67 locations). For the largest new investments, the percentage is even lower at 60 percent (29 locations
in development areas out of the total of 48).

The distribution of the plants by industrial group is shown in
Table 10. These industries or industrial groups are broken down
into seven categories. The chemicals, petroleum, textiles, and food
industries have large enough samples that they can be considered
separately. The metals and metallic fabrications is an industrial

TABLE 10

Industrial Categories and Propensity to Invest
in Depressed Areas

(1)	(2)	(3)	(4)	(5)
		Total Number of New Plant Locations	Total Number of New Plant Locations in Depressed Areas of 1966 Law	Column 4 as a percent of Column 3
Rank	Industry			
1	Textiles	36	31	86
2	Metals and metallic fabrications	81	57	70
3	Chemicals and plastics	37	24	65
4	Food, beverage, tobacco	21	13	62
5	Other industry*	73	43	59
6	Petroleum and Gas	14	7	50
7	Paper and Glass	11	5	45

*This includes the electronics industry, a particularly attractive one from the point of view of the Belgian government. The problem with listing it as a separate category here is that it is yet so small that the Belgian national statistics have no separate electronics category. The industry accounts for only .26 percent of the Belgian GNP as compared with 10 percent for the metals and metallic fabrications, 2.5 percent for chemicals, 2.2 percent for textiles, and 6.2 percent for food. The electronics figure is from Kredietbank Weekly Bulletin, Report on the Belgian Electronics Industry, May 23, 1969, p. 193. The other percentages were calculated by the author from the National Bank of Belgium, Bulletin d'Information et de Documentation, National Bank of Belgium, April, 1969, Table I-3, Gross National Production Calculated by Analysis of Production at Market Prices, p. 462.

Source: Calculated from listings of location of new foreign investment in L'Investissement Etrangers en Belgique, 1967, 1968, 1969, and 1970 reports.

group that was not further subdivided for several reasons.* First,
there was the problem of classification. The author's classification
might not correspond to that utilized by the compilers of the raw data.
Second, certain new plants produced several products in two or more
industries and, without knowledge of the volume of production of each
product, it would be impossible to classify these plants as to their
industry.** Finally, a large number of subdivisions would not provide
a sufficiently large sample for each category with regard to certain
of the statistical tests that were run on the breakdown of these industries to determine the trends in the changes in the industrial structure.***

----

    *An industry is an aggregate of firms producing similar products,
while an industrial group is a group of industries that, although different
in some respects, are similar enough in most respects to be considered
collectively. In fact, by U.S. classification, all of the seven types of
activities would be considered major industrial groups (two digit
classification) and not industries at all. Although the author is aware
of the difference in technical meaning between industrial groups and
industries, industry is used throughout this study to refer to the relatively homogenous activites of textiles, petroleum and natural gas,
chemicals and plastics, and food. The term industrial group will be
used to connote those more diverse activities such as metals and
metallic fabrications. Paper and glass are combined in an industrial
group because two foreign firms produced both products, and the
economic characteristics of the two industries were not widely different with the sole exception of the more labor-intensive aspect of
the glass industry. Finally, the catch-all "other industries" was
added to include all those diverse activities that were not large enough
to stand as their own sample or for which there was not sufficient
statistical data (the electronics industry). For a more complete discussion of the terms "industry" and "industrial group" see W. H.
Miernyk, The Elements of Input-Output Analysis (New York: Random
House, 1969), pp. 17-21.
    **The classification of the most important product in terms of
production determines the industry to which a given establishment of
firm belongs. See Miernyk, The Elements of Input-Output Analysis,
op.cit., pp. 7-8.
    ***See note on page 37 for a discussion of the use of the chi-square
test to discover the significance of the number of plant locations by
industry in 1967 and 1968 for both the total new foreign locations and
those only in depressed areas, and the existing Belgian industrial
structure.

Table 10 also provides data concerning the distribution of the
new plant locations by industry. The tendency to invest in regional
development areas varies from a high of 86 percent for the textile
industry to 45 percent for the paper and glass industry.

The matrix in Table 11 shows the size of plant by type of industry. The total does not equal 273 because, as it may be recalled, the
Belgian statistics do not give the capitalization figure for all new
investments. The figures can be accepted as representative of the
entire sample because a chi-square test was run on the percentage
of depressed plant locations of total plant locations by industry, and
the results were not significant at the 95 percent confidence level.*
The matrix yields no surprising conclusion as to the distribution by
industry of the size of investment. The total rank order industry is
the same as for the total sample, except for the petroleum and chemical industries whose position is reversed. The most noteworthy
observations concern the other industry, food, paper and glass, and
chemical and petroleum categories. The other industry category is
very heavily oriented toward depressed areas in small plants and
much less so in medium and large plants. The food and paper and
glass industries are progressively oriented away from depressed
areas with larger plant size. For chemical and petroleum industries
there is little correlation between propensity to invest in regional
development areas and size of investment.

In much of the remainder of this study, the concentration will
be on the total number of investments and will tend to relegate the
size of these investments to a secondary position. Although it is
obvious that a large new foreign investment will have more influence
on a depressed area than will a smaller one, the approach that concentrates on total new investments has been adopted for three reasons.
First, the relatively small sample size of 48 large and 67 medium
investments when they are divided into the seven industries studied,
would be subject to considerably greater skewness in the statistical

---

*The chi-square test is a test of goodness of fit between two
sets of variables subdivided into categories. The first of these sets
is the proportion that one wishes to test against an existing or true
proportion to determine variance. In this example, the existing
proportion was the percentages of propensity to invest by industry
revealed by the whole sample of 124 locations. The proportion that
was tested against this was the same percentage, but for the industries by size of investment. The value of the chi-square was .047,
whereas the critical value at 95 percent confidence level is 12.59.
See Kong Chu, Principles of Econometrics (Scranton: International
Textbook, 1968), p. 11-13.

TABLE 11

Matrix of Size of Equity Investment and Propensity
to Invest in Depressed Areas

Industry	Size of Investment			
	(depressed locations BF 1-9.9 million (total locations)	BF 10-49.9 million	BF 50 + million	Totals by Industry
Textiles (depressed locations)	20	7	1	28
(total locations)	24	7	1	32
Metals and metallic fabrications	22	19	8	49
	32	28	10	70
Other industry	20	6	8	34
	32	11	16	59
Food	8	2	1	11
	9	2	4	15
Paper and glass	0	4	1	5
	0	5	4	9
Petroleum & gas	1	1	3	5
	3	4	3	10
Chemicals and plastics	9	6	7	22
	12	10	10	32
Total plant size	80	45	29	154
	112	67	48	227

Source: Calculated from individual plant locations by capitalization by author from L'Investissement Etrangers en Belgique, 1967,
1968, 1969, and 1970 reports.

testing than is the total sample of 154 investments. Second, although
one would suppose the effect of one large plant on a depressed area
is larger than one small plant, there are two and a half times more
small plant locations in the sample than there are large ones. In
this circumstance the author felt the adoption of any weighting procedure would be more arbitrary than useful. Third, the only data
available for categorizing the investments by size is the amount of
their equity capital. We are more interested in the total amount

invested, which includes both equity and debt capital. In view of the absence of information regarding total investment or the degree of leverage to be utilized by each new investor, the author was reluctant to base his conclusions on equity investment figures, which might be misleading for total investment.

The primary purpose of this section is to relate the propensity to invest in the regional development areas to the economic characteristics of these industries in order, in the next section, to evaluate the implications for regional development. The remainder of this section continues to discuss industry's characteristics, whereas the next section will link the industries (and their characteristics) to the specific regions. The specific characteristics discussed with relation to an industry's PIRD are size of investment (for the new plants only), profitability, growth in production, productivity, exports, labor intensity, high technology, and proportion of fixed assets to total assets. All of these characteristics, except the last, will be discussed within the specific Belgian context. The selection of these particular economic characteristics was determined by the fact that they are all, except for the size of fixed assets, target variables of the Belgian government.

Profitability and Depressed Area Investment

The profitability of industry has been and remains one of the weaknesses of the Belgian industrial structure in that profits are more important as a source of investable funds than are external funds.* Profits are also very important to the process of external fund raising. Low profits and low cash flow from operations (profits plus depreciation) limit external debt capacity. In addition, constantly low profits hinder the sale of equity for obvious reasons. Expected profitability in the long run is the single most important determinant of future investment—a factor recognized by the Belgian government.

The propensity to investment in depressed areas is inversely correlated with the index of gross profitability (earnings before interest and taxes) by industry. The gross profit index is utilized here because it provides better evaluation of the external debt capacity of the industries than the use of a net profit index. However, the use of a net profit index would not have changed the rankings materially.

------

*For the relation between internal and external sources of funds in the United States and Belgium compared, see Chapter 1, section on Belgian Industrial Structure-Domestic Economy. "Belgian Regional Structure," pp. 9-10.

TABLE 12

Industry's Tendency to Invest in Depressed Areas and
Index of Gross Profitability

Industry	Rank in Propensity to Invest in Depressed Areas	Gross Profitability Index	Profit Rank
Textiles	1	112	7
Metals and metallic fabrications	2	115	6
Chemicals and plastics	3	137	3
Food, beverage, tobacco	4	127	5
Other industry	5	160	1
Petroleum & gas	6	134	4
Paper and glass	7	138	2

Note: Where two industries have been combined into a larger industrial group the profit index figure is a simple average of the component industry figures. The other industry figure is the average figure for all of Belgian industry, except the coal mines.

Source: The gross profit index is from the Kredietbank Weekly Bulletin, published by the Kredietbank, January 28, 1972, pp. 33-39— their annual study of company results in Belgium for the year 1968.

The relation between the propensity to invest in regional development areas and the index of gross profitability is presented in Table 12.

The rank order coefficient of correlation profitability and propensity to invest in depressed regions is -.75 (the coefficient of determination $r2 = .56$.)[21] From this it appears that the firms that most tend to invest in these regions are concentrated in the low-profit industries of Belgium, which implies low future investment potential. While it is generally accepted that American firms earn higher than local rates of profit, the rate of profit in each industry is related to the production function and demand conditions. If the demand facing one's product is low, then even the most efficient combination of inputs (related to management, the ostensible newest American special

TABLE 13

Industry's Tendency to Invest in Depressed Areas
and Its Index of Industrial Production

Industry	Rank in Propensity to Invest in Depressed Areas	1970 Index of Industrial Production	Rank on Industrial Production Index
Textiles	1	109	7
Metals and metallic fabrications	2	141	5
Chemicals and plastics	3	143	4
Food, beverage, tobacco	4	136	6
Other industry	5	165	3
Petroleum and gas	6	177	2
Paper and glass	7	246	1

Source: Index of Industrial Production from National Bank of
Belgium, Bulletin d'Information et de Documentation, November,
1971, Table IV-2, p. 15. The paper and glass figure (simple average
of the two industries) was computed by the author from Ministry of
Economic Affairs L'Economie Belge en 1970, p. 155.

advantage) will not automatically yield a rate of return sufficient to
attract external funding needed for future investment.*

Industrial Growth and Depressed Area Investment

Table 13 presents an index of industrial production for 1968
(1958 = 100). The period is long enough to vary all factor inputs, so
that production is a reflection of demand for the industry's products.22
Industries that have a tendency to invest in depressed areas
also tend to be those industries that face more sluggish demand.

---

*Another and perhaps more convincing reason is that the Ameri-
can firms are a smaller proportion of the less profitable industries
than they are of the total sample. It may be recalled that 58/124
of the locations were American (47 percent). For the textile industry,
it is only 3/12 (25 percent).

In this comparison, as with the comparison with profitability, the correlation is a high inverse one, r = -.89 (r^2 = .79). The relatively high ranking for the metals and metallic fabrications hides two conflicting trends. One is the drop in crude metals and steels, while the other, stronger, trend is the great increase in the metallic fabrications industry, producing such products as motor vehicles and advanced machinery.*

Productivity and Depressed Area Investment

Productivity is one of the key elements in economic growth and is the factor underlying wage levels, propensity to export, and growth rates.[23] A comparison of the PIRD by industry and the productivity for the 1967-68 period of these industries reveals the same inverse correlation as was established for profits and demand. The coefficient of correlation between two variables was r = -.95 (r^2 = .89), which is significant at the 1 percent level. The Belgian national statistics offer no productivity indexes, so the crude productivity index was calculated by the author for all industries except the food industry where there was no data on employment trends.** The productivity

---

*See Chapter 1, section on "Belgian Regional Structure."
**The crude productivity index calculated was the 1968 industrial production index (1958 = 100) minus the employment index for 1968 (1958 = 100) for that industry. The various multi-industry categories (metals and metallic fabrications, glass and paper) are simple averages of their component parts. There is no food productivity index calculated because the author could find no employment index for that industry. The other industry category is the average for Belgian industry. But this double counts those industries already considered separately. If the influence of the textiles and the metal industrial group could be disregarded, both of which were below the average in productivity, then metals and other industries would change ranks and the correlation would be a perfectly inverse one of -1.0. It was not possible to do this because of the impossibility of finding employment indexes for all those industries not considered above.
Interestingly enough, the Belgian government does not publish productivity indexes either in total or by industry in any of its statistical publications, the Bulletin d'Information et de Documentation of the National Bank, the Ministry of Economic Affair's annual L'Economie Belge of Belgium, or the Institute National d'Statistique's monthly Bulletin de Statistique.

index by industry for 1968 (1958 = 100) was 48 for textiles, 55 for metals and metallic fabrications, 54 for other industries, 59 for paper and glass, 90 for chemicals, and 216 for petroleum.

Exports and Depressed Area Investment

Studies in the United States have revealed the close relation between productivity and propensity to export.[24] Normally one would expect that because productivity is so inversely correlated with the propensity to invest in regional development areas the volume export index by industry would have a similar negative correlation. For Belgium this was not the case. The rank order coefficient of correlation between PIRD and the export index is $r = .14$ ($r^2 = .02$). This low correlation is largely explained by two factors. First, the petroleum industry, which ranks high in profit, production, and productivity areas and low in terms of propensity to invest in depressed areas, is primarily engaged in domestic sales. Second, the food industry, which was an average one by the economic tests mentioned above, has had an exceptionally large export volume growth since 1958. The export performance of the food industry also reflects the entrance of large American food corporations into Belgium since 1958.[25]

Table 14 illustrates the relation between an industry's propensity to invest in depressed areas and its export volume index.

TABLE 14

Industry's Tendency to Invest in Depressed Areas
and the 1970 Index of Exports
(1963 = 100)

Industry	Rank in Propensity to Invest in Depressed Areas	Index of Exports	Export Rank
Textiles	1	97	6
Metals and metallic fabrications	2	125	1
Chemicals and plastics	3	102	5
Food, beverage, tobacco	4	118	2
Other industry	5	117	3
Petroleum and gas	6	87	7
Paper and glass	7	104	4

Source: National Bank of Belgium, Bulletin d'Information et de Documentation, November 1971, Table VIII-4, p. 36.

Employment and Depressed Area Investment

One of the symptoms of regional underdevelopment is a high and persistent rate of unemployment. Because certain industries are more labor intensive than others, it follows that this type of industry is more valuable to the regional development process than those that are less labor intensive. The amount of employment created by a foreign investment is one of the most important criteria from the point of view of the Belgian government in deciding the desirability of a given project.*

The relation between an industry's propensity to invest in regional development areas and its labor intensiveness is shown in Table 15.

The coefficient of correlation between the industry's propensity to invest in depressed areas and its labor intensiveness is $r = .21$ ($r^2 = .04$). This was the one correlation that was partially skewed because of the combination of several industries into one industrial group. The relatively low correlation (as compared to those done previously) is accounted for by the labor intensiveness of the glass industry in Belgium, which brought the combined average for the paper and glass industrial group to the second rank and consequently lower than the overall correlation. Excluding the paper and glass industry, the correlation is $r = .60$ ($r^2 = .36$). These correlations may not be indicative of the current situation because the labor intensiveness index is based on 1958 data.

Similarities between the Economic Characteristics of Depressed Area Investments in 1967-68 and Those Taking Place during 1967-70

When an industry's propensity to invest in depressed areas for new foreign investment occurring in 1967-68 is correlated with 1968 data for the various economic characteristics the results are broadly similar to those obtained by correlating investments over the 1967-70 period with 1970 data. For example, the correlation between an industry's depressed area investment rank and its 1968 profitability rank is $r = -.89$ ($r^2 = .79$), which is relative comparable to the $r = -.75$ obtained for the entire 1967-70 sample.

---

*This is shown by the priority given to unemployment in delimiting the original depressed areas. See pp. 18-19 of the section in Chapter 2 on "The Legal Framework of the Investment Incentive Program."

TABLE 15

Industry's Tendency to Invest in Depressed Areas
and Index of Labor Intensity

Industry	Rank in Propensity to Invest in Depressed Areas	Labor Intensive- ness Index	Labor Intensive- ness Rank
Textiles	1	5.49	1
Metals and metallic fabrications	2	2.67	4
Chemicals and plastics	3	2.16	6
Food, beverage, tobacco	4	2.31	5
Other industry	5	2.93	3
Petroleum and gas	6	.67	7
Paper and glass	7	3.02	2

Source: The index of labor intensiveness is taken from an article by W. K. Brauers, "De Opstelling van ein Input-Output Tabel voor de Belgishe Economie in 1958," in Cahiers Economiques de Bruxelles, No. 11, 1st Trimester, 1964. Brauers used the 1958 Belgian input-output table to compute these coefficients of labor intensiveness, which refer to the number of workers necessary to produce a given value of output. The other industry category represents, as with the other correlations, the average of all Belgian industrial industries, excluding the extractive.

Both the 1967-68 and the 1967-70 data showed the industries with the largest tendency to invest in depressed areas were also those industries with the slowest rate of growth in industrial production. The correlation between these two factors was r = -.82 in the 1967-68 period, increasing to r = -.89 for the entire 1967-70 period.

There was little correlation between an industry's depressed area location ranking and its export index ranking. For the 1967-68 sample the correlation was r = -.32, while for the four years between 1967 and 1970, it was r = .14.

The most difficult correlation to explain is that between an industry's depressed area investment rank and that industry's co-efficient of labor intensiveness. For the 1967-68 sample the correlation of r = .71 seemed to indicate that industries selecting a depressed area location were highly labor intensive. However, for

the entire 1967-70 period this correlation declines to r = .21. The
author's opinion is that the correlations may be biased for both samples
and the entire period is likely to be more inaccurate than that of
1967-68 because the coefficient of labor intensiveness is based on
1958 data.

In summation, a comparison of the results obtained by correlating
depressed area investment that took place in 1967-68 and comparing
those taking place during 1967-70 with various economic characteristics indicates there was little shift over time in the economic profile
of the type of industry likely to invest in a Belgian depressed area.
These industries were most likely to have a low rate of profit, a slow
rate of growth in production, and were not export oriented.

Fixed Assets and Depressed Area Investment

There is one final variable that must be examined before this
study can conclude its consideration of the economic characteristics
of those industries that have located new plants in Belgium in 1967
and 1968. It will be recalled that the subsidies are directly related
to the amount of investment for fixed assets of the investing firm.
The most efficient combination of factor inputs for one industry might
contain a much larger percentage of fixed assets to total assets than
is the case for another industry.[26] This means that those industries
that normally have higher fixed asset/total asset ratios would be
more highly subsidized than those with lower similar ratios, given
the same amount of total investment by the different industries.

The relation between the prosperity to invest in regional development areas and the rank order of the net fixed asset/total asset is
shown in Table 16. There is no public information on this ratio for
Belgian industry. The concern here is with foreign investment in
Belgium (the majority of which is American investment) so that the
ratios utilized were computed from the industry averages for U.S.
firms in 1968, under the assumption that Americans making new
investments would utilize the same techniques (i.e., allocations of
assets) and that this ratio would be approximately the same for other
foreign investment as at home.

The coefficient of correlation for the two variables in Table 16
is r = -.79 (r^2 = .62). The weakness of the correlation is shown by
the fact that the industry with the second greatest tendency to invest
in depressed areas has by far the smallest percentage net fixed
assets/total assets. On the other hand, the two industries with the
largest net fixed asset percentage and hence the greatest possible
subsidy (paper and glass, and petroleum) have one of the smallest
propensities to invest in those regions where they could most benefit
from the government's program.

TABLE 16

Industry's Tendency to Invest in Depressed Areas
and Net Fixed Assets as a Percentage of Total Assets

Industry	Rank in Propensity to Invest in Depressed Areas	Net Fixed Assets as a Percentage of Total Assets	Fixed Assets Rank
Textiles	1	35.7	5
Metals and metallic fabrications	2	26.2	7
Chemicals and plastics	3	36.0	4
Food, beverage, tobacco	4	34.7	6
Other industry	5	36.9	3
Petroleum and gas	6	44.7	1
Paper and glass	7	44.5	2

Source: The net fixed assets/total assets percentages were
calculated by industry and averaged to obtain the industrial scores
above by the author. The industry figures were obtained from the
Robert Morris Associates' Annual Statement Studies (Philadelphia,
1969). This is an annual publication representing the average balance-
sheet figures by industry that are contributed to the Robert Morris
Associates for the National Association of Bank Loan and Credit
Officers. The average figure for all sizes of companies was the one
used to compute the industry and industrial group averages. The
other industry figure was the average of the six industries because
there is no average for all industry in the Annual Statement Studies,
1969 edition.

A point that has not yet been discussed is the statistical relation,
in terms of industrial structure, between those new plants in the
depressed areas and those of the total sample. Table 17 presents
the plant locations by industry and the number of plant locations by
industry in depressed areas on a pro rata basis for 124 depressed
area locations.* The statistical relationship between these two

---

*For example, 10 of the total 78 depressed area plant locations
are for the textile industry (13 percent). This 13 percent was then

TABLE 17

Industrial Structure of the Depressed Area
New Investment Locations

Industry	Number of Investments in a Whole Sample	Pro Rata Number of Investments for Depressed Area Locations
Textiles	36	47
Metals and metallic fabrications	81	86
Chemicals and plastics	37	36
Food, beverage, tobacco	21	20
Other industry	73	65
Petroleum and gas	14	11
Paper and glass	11	8

Source: Calculated by the author from listings of individual new investments in L'Investissement Etrangers en Belgique, 1967-70 reports. The pro rata figures for the investment locations in depressed areas were calculated as described in the asterisked note on pp. 47-48.

probability distributions by industry was calculated by the use of the chi-square test. The chi-square result was 5.87 when the critical value at the 5 percent confidence level for six degrees of freedom is 12.59.[27] It may be concluded that there is no statistical difference between the industrial structure represented by the depressed area plant locations and that represented by the entire sample of new investments.

This section has considered the number of new plant locations and the economic characteristics of seven industries and industrial groups in relation to their propensity to invest in the depressed areas (as delimited by the 1966 Law of regional development) in the years 1967 through 1970. It has been seen that 66 percent of the new plant locations (180/273) were made in these regional development areas.

---

multiplied by 124 total plant locations to give a figure of 16 textile plants if the 78 depressed area locations were expanded to 124.

The propensity to invest in these regions declined with the size of the investment from 71 percent for small investments to 67 percent for medium ones and finally to 60 percent for the large category.

The propensity to invest in regional development areas (PIRD) was computed for various industries and industrial groups and this percentage was ranked and correlated with certain economic characteristics that the Belgian government regards as important in the regional development process. These included the correlations between the PIRD and the economic characteristics of size of investment, profitability, production (reflecting demand for the industry's products in the long run), exports, productivity, and the percentage of total assets that are comprised of fixed assets.

The study of economic characteristics associated with a new investment in one of the 1966 depressed areas would show that the new investment would probably be small in a relatively unprofitable, nontechnological industry facing low demand and with low productivity. The new investment probably also would be labor intensive, although this is not clear because the labor intensiveness index utilized was based on 1958 data. The new investment would export about as much as other new investments that did not locate in depressed areas. In addition, the reason for the selection of a depressed area as a plant location site in all likelihood was not strongly influenced by the fixed assets aspects of the incentive laws that determine the amount of subsidy. Finally, it was shown that the industrial structure of the entire sample was not statistically different from its depressed area component.

IMPLICATIONS OF THE INVESTMENT LOCATIONS ON BELGIAN REGIONAL DEVELOPMENT

In this section the sectoral industrial analysis of the previous section will be applied to the individual Belgian regions. The section has four points of reference:

1. To what extent has the 1966 Law attracted greater total foreign investment and to what extent has the Law redistributed this total among the regions than had previously been the case.

2. A study of the effects of certain exogenous economic variables, such as tariffs, on the regional development process.

3. The effect of the investment incentives program on the regional development of the various individual provinces. This studies the interrelation between the industries and their characteristics and the Belgian provinces referred to above.

4. Other locational considerations for foreign investment.

Distributional Effects

We have already seen that American investment in Belgium is growing at a faster rate than is the average for the EEC (see "Introduction" to this chapter). Because American investment is by far the largest portion of foreign investment in all of the EEC countries, it is probable that Belgium's index of foreign investment is also increasing at a more rapid rate than is the European average.

Two primary reasons for Belgium's success in attracting foreign investment are first, and least important, that the investment-creating effects of a common market in a small country such as Belgium are probably slight at the beginning of a market whose final tariffs are arrived at by gradual stages. The investment-creating effects are not complete until internal duties have been abolished and the common external duties are effective.*

The second reason concerns political attitudes of the host governments of the member countries. Recent research has shown that the investment climate is one of the factors making a given country relatively attractive to foreign investment.[28] One of the principal components of investment climate is government attitude toward foreign investment. In a common market, this means that a foreign firm can pick the country that is most favorable toward foreign investment and still enjoy the trade with the partner economies.[29] A third important reason, favorable central geographic location, is discussed later in this chapter.

The EEC case has shown that foreign firms tend to "shop around" for the best deal from host governments. When investment conditions for foreign investment (which is mainly American) began to appear less favorable in the three major countries, the result has been to increase American interest in those remaining member countries with friendly investment climates. The situations in Germany, France, and Italy are too complicated to be recounted here in depth, but their ramifications increased American interest in Belgium.[30]

The conclusion is that the rise in the rate of foreign investment in Belgium relative to that of the rest of the Common Market is not

---

*This argument was further elaborated in the "Introduction" to this chapter. This investment-creating effect is limited as it tacitly assumes that investors do not anticipate these changes. In fact, investments are made on the basis of expected return, which would incorporate the investors anticipation of tariff changes. For this reason the author's opinion is that the attitude and actions of the Belgian government has had paramount importance in attracting foreign investment to Belgium and away from the other EEC countries.

directly related to the 1966 investment incentive program per se.
There is an indirect relation inasmuch as the government's investment
incentive program reflects its desire to maintain a favorable investment climate for foreign investment.

The location of foreign investment between the depressed and
normal regions of Belgium has changed since 1961. Jacques Hollander's
book shows a map of American investments in Belgium between 1957
and 1961.[31] A comparison of this period with 1967 and 1968 presents
both differences and similarities. The differences are in the overall
propensity to invest in depressed areas and in the concentration of
new investments around certain urban locations. Only 35 of the 99
(35 percent) new investments were located in the depressed regions
specified by the Regional Development Law of July 18, 1959.[32] This
is considerably below the 63 percent figure from the 1967-68 sample,
and the 66 percent from the entire 1967-70 data. In addition, the
earlier period shows a much heavier concentration of new investment
in the Brussels and Antwerp urban regions. The number of new
investments in those two urban areas dropped from 41 percent (41 of
99 new investments) in the 1957-61 period to 20 percent (25/123) in
1967-68.[33]

The most important similarity seems to be that the individual
industries, of tendency to invest in depressed areas has remained
the same, despite the higher percentage of total investment going into
depressed areas in 1967-68. For the textile industry, for example,
7 of 10 new investments in the earlier period were made in depressed
areas. For the metals and metallic fabrications the tendency to invest
in regional development areas was 43 percent (9 of 21 investments
were in the 1959 depressed areas), a figure well above the average
for the entire sample of 35 percent. In the 1967-70 period the textile
industry and metals and metallic fabrications were the only two industries having a greater tendency to invest in depressed areas than the
average for all industries. The textile figure was 86 percent, the
metals and metallic fabrications, 70 percent, and the national average,
66 percent.[34]

The author's opinion is that this improvement in the percentage
of new investments in depressed areas is based on three factors that,
either directly or indirectly, relate to the government's program
for regional development. The first is the moral suasion of the
government in trying to convince foreign firms to locate in the depressed areas. The second is the effect of the 1966 Law itself, which
expanded both the effective rate of the subsidy and the geographic
regions over which it is payable. Third, some of the industries that
have a high tendency to locate in depressed areas would not have
done so without the subsidies. For these industries, the increase
in rate of subsidy and the geographical area defined as depressed

may provide a "windfall" benefit. The economic characteristics of
the industries that tend to locate in regional development areas are
low productivity, low profits, and stagnant demand. This type of
industry in a developed country such as Belgium also tends to be
labor intensive as a result of technological limitations.[35] Regional
development areas, whether or not they are formally recognized and
subsidized by the host government, usually have higher unemployment
and lower wage rates than other regions. Lower wage rates attract
labor intensive industries.[36] This positive aspect is limited by two
negative factors. The first is the principle of diminishing marginal
rate of factor substitution. The second is that there are transport,
marketing, and other variable costs that tend to rise with plant location
in disadvantaged areas.* The effect on total costs for the depressed
area investor depends on whether the net effect from these three
factors is positive or negative.

The 1966 Law increased the size of the depressed areas eligible
for investment incentives. If a new investment is labor intensive
the 1966 Law provides much larger regional choices for the investment
to benefit from the lower wages in depressed areas, accept the subsidy,
and yet limit its additional costs resulting from a less advantageous
position because so much of Belgium has been declared a depressed
area. Hence, for a labor intensive industry the extension over a
larger geographic area provided an inducement to invest that was not
present with the smaller official depressed areas of 1959.

Two conclusions are that, (1) the investment incentive program
had little weight in attracting investment to Belgium, and (2) there
was a substantial change in the distribution of foreign investment
coming into Belgium between the normal and depressed areas between
the late 1950s and 1968. The marginal increase in the size of subsidies available and the marginal reduction of the difference in attract-
tiveness between optimal depressed and nondepressed locations
(because of the increase in size of the depressed areas) accounted
for the investor's greater tendency to invest in depressed areas in
1967-70 relative to 1958-62. The author's conclusion is that this
distributional change was primarily a result of the 1966 Regional
Development Law that increased both the amount of incentives and
the areas over which they are payable.

---

*This analysis omits the possibility of either external economies
or diseconomies because the author has not found information concerning these with regard to Belgium that would permit meaningful
analysis.

Exogenous Economic Considerations

Exogenous economic variables may have harmful consequences for a regional development program. They are exogenous variables because they are not under the direct and final control of the host government. These variables tend to increase in importance in situations, such as common markets, that involve more than one country. Specifically with regard to Belgium and the EEC there are two such variables that merit investigation. The first is the authority of the EEC as a whole to limit the investment incentive program of a member country. The second is a consideration of the real tariff rates of the industries that have the highest propensity to invest in depressed areas.

The executive organs of the EEC are empowered by Article 92 of the Treaty of Rome to limit the amount of aid given by member states to foreign investments. This is possible in situations where the EEC deems the giving of such aid would distort competition between members by giving an unfair advantage to the company receiving the subsidy.[37] The only adverse ruling taken by the EEC on these grounds to date was a case in Belgium. In 1964 the Belgian government expressed the intention to give the Ford Tractor Company (Belgium) in Antwerp the interest rate rebate granted in accordance with the General Aid provisions of the Law of July 17, 1959. The EEC decided on October 28, 1964, after an examination of the project plans and a consideration of the difficulties experienced by member-country companies in that industry, that the Belgian government must withdraw its aid.[38] Although this single example has been the only case of its type, it is clear from the Treaty of Rome that the EEC could be a restraining influence on the unilateral application of regional development programs by a member state.

The second consideration is that of the effects of tariff policy upon new investments in regional development areas. A national government can affect the growth of a region by its tariff policy. A low rate of effective protection for an industry that is not competitive internationally but has a high tendency to invest in depressed areas could have a harmful effect on a depressed areas program.[39]

In the Belgian case the situation is more complicated because the Belgian government no longer uniquely determines the tariff rates for Belgium. It is possible that the tariff rates for Belgium, determined by the EEC, do, in fact, discriminate against those industries that have shown the greatest tendency to invest in depressed areas. In this situation the policy decided on the Community level could conflict with national policy.

The relation between the propensity to invest by industry in the depressed areas set up by the 1966 Law (the 1967-70 investment

locations) and the real rate of tariffs these industries is shown in
Table 18.[40] The real tariff rate for each industry is calculated by
dividing that industry's total tariff duties paid by its total value added
at market prices. The classes of industries are highly aggregated
both because the small size of the sample would not allow statistically
significant disaggregation and because the listing of the individual
firms by location is unclear in certain cases concerning the subindustry
into which certain firms should be placed. In view of the highly
aggregated nature of these classes, the conclusions derived from the
statistical analysis cannot be regarded as definitive.

The rank order coefficient of correlation between the PIRD and
the real tariff rate is $r = .04$, which indicates that EEC tariff policy
has not adversely affected those industries that had the greatest
tendency to invest in Belgian depressed areas. It is possible that the
advent of the Common Market has benefited certain industries because
of the greater availability of factor inputs from member countries

TABLE 18

Industry's Tendency to Invest in Depressed Areas
and Its Real Tariff Rate

Industry	Rank in Propensity to Invest in Depressed Areas	Real Tariff Rate = Duties Paid/ Value Added (in percent)	Rank of Real Tariff Rate
Textiles	1	10.2	4
Metals and metallic fabrications	2	9.8	3
Chemicals and plastics	3	11.5	6
Food, beverages, tobacco	4	5.5	7
Other industry	5	10.7	5
Petroleum and gas	6	19.2	7
Paper and glass	7	7.9	2

Source: The percentage real tariff rates were calculated from
the 1959 Belgian input-output table released by the Office Statistique
des Communautes Europeenes, Tableaux "Entrees-Sorties" pour les
pays de la Communaute Europeene Economique, October, 1964. The
percentages reflect the total duty on imports paid as a percentage
of total value added at market price.

that would be lower in cost than other inputs from outside the EEC. It is equally possible to assume that the trade-diversion effects of the Common Market have resulted in approximately equal cost increments for all industries resulting from either the higher common external tariff (in the case of Belgium) on inputs from outside the EEC or the diversion of input purchases from the outside to higher cost member countries because of the higher tariff.

The conclusion of this discussion of the exogenous variables is that these variables have had little influence on that program. The EEC High Commission clearly has the legal right to limit member government subsidy programs that give unfair competitive advantage to a foreign firm resident in that country. This right has been used only one time and that was with reference to a proposed subsidy to be given in one of the most dynamic growth regions of Belgium. This cannot be considered as an impediment to the Belgian regional development program.

The second exogenous variable, tariff policy, has also had a minor role upon the regional program. There is no correlation between the industries that have the highest propensity to invest in depressed areas and the weight of the tariffs they have to pay. It is doubtful whether this factor has had a large harmful effect on the regional development program, although this analysis is limited by the use of industry groupings that are too aggregated.

Effects of the 1966 Investment Incentive Program

The connection between the various industries and the tendency to invest in various provinces is presented in matrix form in Table 19. The figure in the upper left-hand corner of each cell refers to the number of new investments of that industry and province that are located in the 1966 depressed areas. The number in the lower right-hand corner refers to the total number of new foreign investments in that industry or province in 1967 and 1968.

It is clear from the matrix that the provinces that have had the most success attracting new foreign investment into their 1966 depressed areas are Liege and Hainaut. Hainaut received 55 new investments in the 1967-70 period, 53 that were in depressed areas. Liege received 56 new foreign investments in these two years and 54 of these were in depressed areas. The provinces of Antwerp and Brabant also had large numbers of new foreign investments, but registered a much lower proportion in regional development areas. This figure was 36 percent for Antwerp (15 of its 42 foreign investments were in depressed areas) and only 6 percent for Brabant, which was the lowest percentage in Belgium (only 2 investments of the total of 33

TABLE 19

Matrix of Foreign Investment in Regional Development Areas by Industry and by Province

Industry		Antwerp	W. Flanders	E. Flanders	Brabant	Limburg	Liege	Hainaut	Luxembourg	Namur	Totals by Industry
					Province						
Textiles	(depressed locations)	5	6	4	0	9	4	3	0	0	31
	(total locations)	5	8	5	2	9	4	3	0	0	36
Metals and metallic fabrications		4	1	1	0	4	24	19	2	2	57
		12	3	4	8	4	25	19	2	4	81
Other industry		2	3	2	1	9	12	13	1	0	43
		8	7	9	11	9	13	14	2	0	73
Food		1	1	0	1	3	3	2	1	1	13
		4	2	0	5	3	3	2	1	1	21
Paper and glass		0	1	0	0	0	2	2	0	0	5
		2	1	1	3	0	2	2	0	0	11
Petroleum		0	0	1	0	1	2	3	0	0	7
		2	2	3	1	1	2	3	0	0	14
Chemicals		3	0	1	0	2	7	11	0	0	24
		9	0	4	3	2	7	12	0	0	37
Totals by province		15	12	9	2	28	54	53	4	3	180
		42	23	26	33	28	56	55	5	5	273
Propensity to invest in regional development areas by province (in percent)*		36	52	35	6	100	96	96	80	60	66
Percent of total provincial new investment of total for Belgium**		15	8	10	12	10	21	20	2	2	100

*These percentages are the depressed area locations in each province divided by the total new location in that province.
**These percentages are the total locations in a province divided by the total for Belgium.

Sources: New foreign investment locations calculated by author from lists of new investment locations in the 1967-70 reports of L'Investissement Etranger en Belgique. These were broken down by industry and province to create the matrix above:

were in distressed areas). The provinces of East and West Flanders
had close to their pro rata share of new investment with 26 and 23
locations respectively.* The two provinces of Luxembourg and Namur
received much less new investment with only 10 investments between
the two provinces.

The location of the new textile establishments is overwhelmingly
in the Flemish parts of Belgium. The depressed sections of Antwerp,
East Flanders, West Flanders, and Limburg account for 24 of the
total 31. The metals industrial group is most concentrated in Hainaut,
Liege, and Antwerp provinces, with practically all the investment
locations in this group for the first two provinces in the 1966 depressed
areas. The food industry is particularly centered near Antwerp and
Brussels, with 9 of the 21 locations in these provinces. The chemicals
industry has a high propensity to locate near Antwerp. The paper and
glass, petroleum, and other industry industrial groups have a provincial
distribution that approximately parallels the provincial distribution
of the entire sample.

Now that the structure, characteristics, and distribution have
been considered, two other questions must be discussed before conclusions concerning the success of the Belgian program can be drawn.
These two questions have to do with the welfare effect and growth
effects of the new foreign investment. The equalization of provincial
welfare (the welfare effect) clearly is best brought about by increasing
the investment, hence the employment, wages, and purchasing power,
in the poorer provinces relative to the more affluent. The second
question concerns the comparison of growth effects on the regional
and national levels.

The concept of provincial welfare is a vague one. The author
has attempted to give it substance with the computation of a social
benefit rank by province for Belgium by the summation of the provincial rankings of three vital components of the economic welfare of
any geographic entity. The three are the provincial rankings in the
percentage of unemployment, the gross provincial product per capita,
and the provinces' rank on a synthetic welfare index.[41] The social
benefit rank for each province is a criteria for welfare ranking
which includes both income and unemployment figures and the synthetic

---

*By pro rata share the author means that number of investments
that would locate in each province if the total new investments were
equally distributed among the nine provinces. This share is then
273/9 = 30 investments per province, if all the locations were equally
distributed.

welfare index that contrasts various social welfare (education levels) and household use of capital goods.*

One goal of the regional development program is to close the real welfare gap among the provinces. With relation to foreign investment, this could be best accomplished if the new plants were to locate in those provinces with the lowest welfare rank to the detriment of those with the highest welfare rankings. To test the extent to which this has happened between 1967 and 1970 with the new foreign investments the welfare index was compared with the provincial rankings that were based on the number of total new investments in each province. Then the same test was run again but the provincial inverse welfare rankings were correlated with the provincial rankings of investment only in the depressed areas.** In fact, for the entire sample, the rank order coefficient of correlation was r = .01, indicating no statistical relations between provincial welfare and the location of the new investments.*** This is to be expected because this correlation concerns the relation between the inverse provincial welfare index

---

*This composite method was selected because it gives a conception of nominal buying power (the per capita income figure), job security and industrial demand for labor (the unemployment rate), and various other social and other economic variables (the synthetic welfare index) with which one can make real interprovincial comparisons. The rankings in all three components were surprisingly close for most provinces. Brabant was first in all three and Limburg was last. Most of the other provinces had the same rankings on at least two of the ranking criteria. The welfare rankings by province were 1. Brabant, 2. Namur, 3. Antwerp, 4. Liege, 5. Luxembourg, 6. West Flanders, 7. Hainaut, 8. East Flanders, 9. Limburg. The inverse welfare rankings, of course, would rank the provinces in exactly the opposite order, with Limburg as 1 and Brabant as 9.

**The reason for the inverse welfare index is that this is a study of regional depressed areas. These depressed areas are normally found in provinces that would have a low rank in the welfare index. Because the focus of the study is on these low-rank regions, the author felt it appropriate to reverse the welfare rank in order to rank highest those provinces that are most central to the study. This procedure also has the benefit of clarity because a positive correlation between the inverse welfare rank and the number of investment locations by province would indicate that the effect of the foreign investment has been toward equalization of Belgian provincial welfare.

***Here, as with the previous rank order correlations, the ties in number of new investments by province were resolved by splitting the ranks. Hence, for the total sample correlation, the provinces of Antwerp, Liege, and Hainaut, which all had 24 new foreign investments were all given the rank of two.

and the entire sample of new investments, only some of which were induced by the regional development program in the 1966 depressed areas.

The pattern of plant locations in the depressed areas of the 1966 Laws indicates a tendency toward the equalization of provincial welfare between the more affluent provinces and those in the middle of the group, but the poorest are relatively unaffected by the new foreign investments. The rank order correlation between the inverse welfare index and the provincial location of the 180 depressed plant locations is $r = .50$ ($r^2 = .25$). This would indicate that there is some relation between the pattern of the new foreign investment in the depressed areas of the various provinces and the equalization of provincial welfare. The low correlation is accounted for by the fact that the provinces that benefited most from the new investments in their depressed areas were not those lowest ranking in welfare. Hainaut had the largest number of investments in its depressed areas (24), closely followed by Liege (23), but Hainaut is only the third poorest province in terms of welfare, while Liege is the sixth. Conversely, the province that had the second highest rank on the inverse welfare rank, East Flanders, was third from last in terms of the number of new investments within its depressed regions. From this analysis it would appear that, given the government's goal of more equitable provincial welfare, the investment incentive program did not result in a tendency toward the income equalization of the poorest with the richest provinces. Instead, the effect was toward the equalization of those regions that are well situated geographically in terms of transport and market and yet still benefited from the provisions of the 1966 Laws.

For the province with the lowest welfare rank, East Flanders, the effect of new foreign investments has been a relatively worse position in all three components of the social benefit rankings. It has already been seen that there is a strong inverse correlation between variables such as profitability, productivity, and demand and propensity to invest in the depressed areas. Conversely, those firms of a given industry that tend to select locations in the depressed areas are more labor intensive than those that invest in normal regions. The result is that the marginal revenue product, and hence the wages, are lower in those industries that have a high propensity to invest in depressed areas.[42] Because there was no correlation between the inverse welfare index and the investment by province in the total sample it would appear that the final effect on the distribution of provincial income would not be to decrease the inequalities that already exist, given that the industries locating in the normal regions tend to pay higher wages. This change in income will in the long run affect the synthetic welfare index so that the result of foreign investment will not be to narrow the provincial discrepancies materially.

The third component of welfare is employment. The result of
the regional development program has been to decrease the rate of
unemployment in these less affluent provinces, because labor intensive
industries tend to locate in the depressed areas. Here the problem
is that most foreign investment does not locate in those provinces
that are lowest in welfare rankings, so the provinces that most benefit
from favorable employment aspects of investment incentive program
are not those in which the social benefit of higher employment would
be the greatest.

The conclusion is that given the three components of the social
benefits index, the new foreign investment has probably not increased
the income and synthetic index of the lowest ranking provinces relative
to their affluent neighbors. The employment benefit, the third social
benefit, of those industries that have a high propensity to locate in
depressed areas has had a positive result in depressed areas, but
this result is much more marked in the depressed areas of the medium
welfare rank provinces than those of the least affluent provinces.

A second major question concerns the interrelation between the
induced investments in the depressed areas and the regional growth
of the provinces. This is approached most frequently using either
regional multiplier analysis or regional input-output tables.[43] The
problem here is that the regional input-output studies of Belgium
have concentrated only on certain areas.[44] There has been no work
attempting to derive a regional or provincial multiplier in Belgium,
and even if there had been, the results would have been suspect, given
the insufficiency of the provincial data base.[45] If the traditional
form of the multiplier that is normally applied to regional analysis
is accepted there are some conclusions that can be deduced from the
information that has already been discussed. The regional multiplier
for the foreign investment that results in an increase in regional
income dY may be written in the following manner:

$$dY = d \ (I + X) \ \frac{1}{s + m}$$

where dY = increase in regional product
     dI = total amount of the foreign investment
     dX = total amount of exports
     s   = marginal propensity to save for the depressed region
     m   = marginal propensity to import for depressed region.[46]

First assume that $s_r < s_n$, which is the normal case of low income
regions and that $m_r > m_n$, where the r and n refer to the region in
question and the entire nation respectively. It is very probable that
the more severely depressed the region the greater will be the diver-
gence between the two inequalities above. It is also true that the

marginal propensity to import will be considerably larger for the
poorest provinces that contain the worst depressed areas because
they have very little industry, have received very little of the new
foreign investment, and hence, can produce very few of their own
consumption products. If $s_r = 1/10$ and $m_r = 3/5$ for a very poor
province, the multiplier for the province is 1.43. If we assume $s_r =$
$1/6$ and $m_r = 2/6$ for a more prosperous province, then the multiplier
is 2.0.[47] Given these reasonable assumptions concerning the behavior
of s_r and m_r, one would expect the multiplier to be lower in the poorer
provinces.*

The fact that income of a depressed region increases less per
given size investment than does that of a normal region does not
mean that depressed area investment necessarily leads to lower
national growth rates.[48] For example, it is possible that the main
leakage of the regions, the marginal propensity to import, consists
primarily of imports from other provinces, which contribute to their
growth. From the multiplier evidence presented, the author is

---

*The other variable in the multiplicand is the amount of exports.
There has been no study of Belgian regional trading patterns upon
which to base a discussion of the relation of the amount of regional
exports to the propensity to invest in depressed areas of the various
industries. Any assumptions that could be made about this aspect of
the multiplier would be on far shakier ground than any of those made
above. Because of this fact the author has accepted the principle of
the equal distribution of ignorance rule from Bayes' Postulate and
assumed that the amount of regional exports is a neutral factor in the
multiplier effects of the new foreign investment. But even assuming
that X is neutral for all firms regardless of their propensity to invest
in depressed areas, regional exports by those industries with high
PIRD's will tend to be lower. This is true because of the economic
characteristics of the various industries. With a given instrument I,
the industries that have smaller propensity to invest in depressed
areas will have larger output Y because they are more the productive
industries. Hence, assuming the same size investment I for two
industries and also assuming neutral treatment of exports (i.e., that
the same percentage X of exports from the region is made of the
total production Y of the firm), the amount of X will be greater for
those firms that can produce the greatest Y with the given investment
I. Because productivity is inversely related to an industry's propensity to invest in depressed areas, the X for industries that have the
greatest tendency to locate in depressed areas will be lower than
that for the industries that usually select plant sites in normal areas.

reluctant to draw conclusions concerning the effects of depressed area investments on national growth. This brief analysis does suggest the possibility that, given a smaller depressed area than normal area multipliers, equalization of the amounts of depressed area investment with normal area investment will not lead to the equalization of provincial income. It was also probable, assuming the previous relations between the marginal propensities to save an import, that the size of the multiplier in the most depressed areas will also tend to be smaller. The total growth effects of the new foreign investment will tend to be smaller for the depressed regions and provinces.* This suggests the growth effects may even work against the government's goal of equalization of provincial income.

Other Locational Considerations

The decision to invest in a regional development area by a foreign investor involves a calculation of many variables, only one of which is the subsidy given by the government. This section is a brief discussion of certain of the other primary locational variables within the Belgian context.

It has already been seen that for a labor intensive industry the low wage rates normally associated with depressed regions offer an incentive to select such a region even without a government incentive. The textile industry in particular is unusually sensitive to wage differentials when selecting investment locations.[49]

---

*This relation between future reinvestment and growth is more clearly stated in mathematical form. Because low profitability has an inhibiting effect on future investment, then the present value amount of regional growth foregone by an investment in relatively unprofitable industry (I_u) instead of an equal investment in the more profitable industry (I_p) is represented by the following formula:

$$GF = \sum_{n=1}^{\infty} \frac{\left(I_p = I_d\right)^n k}{(1 + r)^n}$$

where GF = the present value of regional growth
    I_p = investment in profitable industry (sum of stream of future investments)
    I_d = sum of stream of future low profit investments
    n = number of years of future investment flows
    r = social discount rate
    k = regional multiplier.

The comparative wage levels between regions, although an important contributing factor, is obviously not the predominant one in Belgium because the depressed areas in the provinces with the lowest wage rates, such as Limburg, received very little new foreign investment.

Another important locational consideration is transport cost, which reflects both nearness to suppliers and to markets. The geographic size of Belgium combined with the selection of relatively large depressed areas has had a positive effect on the 1966 incentive program because a foreign investor can receive a subsidy and still be relatively centrally located.

The selection of Belgium as an investment location is a logical one for foreign investments intending to export much of their production to other EEC countries.[50] The central geographic position of Belgium, relative to the two largest member-country markets tends to minimize transport costs. In addition, the small size of Belgium and the large size of the designated depressed areas within Belgium means that a foreign investor can locate in a depressed area and still be close to market areas. There are, for example, depressed areas within 25 kilometers of Antwerp. Finally, the costs of transport in Belgium tend to be lower than elsewhere in Europe.[51] This means that not only do goods have to be transported a shorter distance between Belgian depressed areas and their destinations than might be the case in other larger political units, but that the per-unit costs of this transport is also lower in Belgium.

The designation of larger regions in Belgium and the increasing of the amount of subsidy available in these regions has diverted more investment into depressed regions than did the previous programs. The distribution of investments among provinces has not been uniform because the depressed areas of the less affluent provinces received less than their share of total depressed area investment. This implies that more graduated incentives for depressed area investment might be a workable method toward the equalization of provincial income.

Locational considerations, other than the investment incentive program itself, appear to have played an important part in the success of the Belgian 1966 regional development program. In addition to the large size of the designated depressed areas relative to the small size of Belgium, location of that country within the EEC has meant that foreign investors could locate in depressed areas, receive government subsidies, and still minimize wage and transport costs to an extent that would not be possible in a larger country.

CONCLUSION

In order to draw conclusions about the Belgian investment incentive program we must first review the aims of the government and see to what extent they were fulfilled. As presented in Chapter 2, the four criteria for Exception Aid (which is the only kind that can be given in the 1966 delimited depressed areas) are:

1. Operations that assure a large diversification of economic activity
2. Operations that favor the establishment of new rapid growth or high value-added industries
3. Operations that provide work for the available manpower by reinforcing and revalorizing as much as possible its occupational qualifications
4. Operations that promote scientific research.[52]

As has been seen, the reaction of new foreign investment to the incentive program has been very favorable as is proven by the fact that 66 percent of the sample of 273 new foreign investments were located in the 1966 depressed areas. However, the economic characteristics of the industries that have the greatest tendency to locate in the depressed areas do not fulfill the four criteria of the Belgian government, except for the employment criterion.

The economic characteristics of the industries that have the highest propensity to invest in regional development areas are almost the opposite of the aims of the government's program. It has been seen that textiles and the metals group are the most prone to investing in depressed areas. These are two of the most traditional sectors in the Belgian industrial structure and would seem to add little to the diversification of economic activity. It has also been noted that there is an almost perfect inverse correlation between the propensity to invest in a distressed area by a given industry and the rate of growth of that industry. It is almost certain that traditional, low profit, low growth industries with high depressed area investment tendencies would conduct very little scientific research.[53]

The consistency of the goals of the program is also questionable. The study has shown that there is an inverse relationship in Belgium between the tendencies of high-growth industry and labor intensive industry to invest in depressed areas. It is possible that by selecting incompatible goals such as the promotion of both high growth industry and labor intensive industry the government has attempted to accomplish more than can reasonably be expected from a single program with a relatively fixed range of subsidies. The author's opinion is that increased flexibility in the program relative to the incentives offered and the regions in which they are available would better promote the divergent goals proclaimed by the government.

The primary success of the 1966 Law has been in attracting a greater share of new foreign investment into depressed areas than did the Law of 1959. As has been seen in the period 1967-68, 66 percent of new foreign investments located in depressed areas, whereas only 35 percent selected a depressed area location in 1958-61. The author's contention is that the marginal distributional effect observed in the latter period resulted from the increased flexibility in the 1966 Law that provided for larger subsidies payable over larger areas.

This distributional effect is less satisfactory when consideration is given to the individual depressed areas. The study showed that most of the new investment was being made in depressed areas located in provinces with an average or higher income and material welfare rank than the national level. The depressed areas in the less affluent provinces received very little foreign investment. The author's belief is that increased flexibility in the program would work, as it has in the past, toward the inducement of more foreign investment into the depressed areas of the less affluent provinces.

From the study of the relation between the tendency to invest in depressed areas and from the economic characteristics of the industries concerned, one concludes that the Belgian government has succeeded in subsidizing defensive investment as defined by Alexandre Lamfalussy.[54] The two characteristics of industries where there are defensive investments are falling or low profit rates and stagnant demand.* The possible negative effect that defensive investment has on national and regional growth may be inferred from Lamfalussy's work.**

It is possible that future tariff policy, which was shown to have little historical impact on Belgian regional development, could have a larger impact. With the increasing emphasis by less developed countries on tariff preferences for their products in developed country markets, it is clear that the conclusions drawn earlier concerning the historical lack of relation between Belgian tariff policy and the industries that have a high propensity to invest in depressed areas might well have to be revised in the future.[55] A substantial lowering of the EEC exterior tariff for exports of less developed countries' textile products could have serious negative effects on the Belgian regional development program.

In conclusion, the Belgian regional incentive program, initiated by the Law of July 14, 1966, has been only a qualified success. The

---

*For example, in this case, the rank order coefficient of multiple correlation between the tendency of firms to invest in depressed areas on one hand and their profit and growth performance on the other, is -.97 ($R^2 = .95$), which is significant at the 1 percent level.

**Lamfalussy does not use formal multiplier methods to analyze defensive investment; he believes its effects on economic growth are negative.

program has been successful in increasing the allocation of new
foreign investment and attracting labor intensive industries to the
depressed areas. It has had considerably less success in attracting
high-growth, research-intensive industries to depressed areas.
Finally, although the program has increased the percentage of foreign
investment going to depressed areas, the individual depressed areas
benefiting from this increase have been those in moderately affluent
provinces, while the depressed areas of the less affluent provinces
have received little new foreign investment.

INVESTMENT INCENTIVES
AS RESOURCE ALLOCATION
DEVICES

Before proceding to a detailed discussion of which type of subsidy is more efficient from the point of view of both the host government and the foreign investor, it is useful to touch briefly upon the
theory of why governments give subsidies to investors. In theory,
a subsidy should be given to a project when the present value of the
social benefits arising from the project is greater than its social
cost. Extensive literature has developed to discuss the proper application of this theory to various types of government programs—from
waterway and manpower studies to World Bank projects.[1]
The most prevalent type of resource allocation theory stresses
the easily quantifiable benefits and costs of government subsidies
while tending to ignore the external economies and diseconomies of
such action. An approach to this type of benefit-cost analysis relating
to the subject of this study was taken by C. W. Hale.[2] In his article,
Hale presents the following formula, slightly modified by the author,
for establishing the benefit-cost ratio for a government subsidy given
to promote investment in a depressed area.

$$r = \sum_{n=i}^{\infty} \frac{\dfrac{K(y + w - L)p}{(1 + i_d)^n}}{S_s + \dfrac{S_m}{(1 + i_d)^n}}$$

where r = the benefit-cost ratio
       K = the regional multiplier
       p = the probability that the subsidy determined the investment
           location in the depressed area

69

S_s = the amount of a subsidy paid in the first year of investment
S_m = the annual amount of a multiperiod investment
i_d = the social discount rate
y = the annual value of the payroll of the new investment
w = the annual dollar reduction in welfare and unemployment
        payments because of employment opportunities offered
        by the new investment
L = the leakages from the payroll in the form of payments to
        other regions or the lower wages forgone by those previ-
        ously employed workers who will now work for higher
        wages included in y above
n = the investment life of the project in years.

In this analysis the social primary benefits are the plant's payroll and a reduction in welfare and unemployment costs. The costs
consist of the payments that are made out of the region, wages forgone
by those previously employed workers who obtain employment at the
new plant, and the amount of the subsidy payments. Since both
benefits and costs take place over the life of the investment, a discount
rate representing the government's use of funds, the social rate of
discount, should be used to present value all benefits and costs. The
social rate of discount is briefly discussed later in this chapter.

The benefit-cost derived by using the formula is an expression
of the present value of the social benefits as compared to the social
costs.

The decision rule for the use of benefit-cost analysis is that if
the ratio of the benefits to the costs is greater than 1:1 then the
investment should be subsidized. For example, if the present value
of social benefits is \$10.2 million, while the present value of social
costs is \$11.7 million, the benefit-cost ratio of .87 $\left(\dfrac{10.2}{11.7}\right)$ is less than

the minimally acceptable ratio. In this instance, the social benefits
are less than the social costs so that the investment should be rejected.

The primary criticism of this approach to government resource
allocation is that it ignores certain costs and benefits that are real
but difficult to quantify. Examples of such costs might include considerations of the extent to which the new investment will contribute
to pollution of the host country's air and water or create traffic jams
requiring further government infrastructure investment. An example
of a benefit that is difficult to quantify is the positive effect on family
stability that arises by employing the previously unemployed. In
summation, it is clear that the traditional approach, by concentrating
on quantifiable variables, may misallocate government resources by
failing to take into consideration the external economics and diseco-
nomics of the new investment.

Government and private investment analysis both apply a discount
rate reflecting the opportunity cost of the resources employed to

establish the present value benefit or cost of making the investment. For the private investor this opportunity cost of resources employed is the company's cost of capital rate, which is briefly discussed in Chapter 7. For the government this opportunity cost is the social rate of discount. As was shown in Hale's formula, the social rate of discount is used to present value the social benefits and costs of the investment. The purpose of this section is to give an operational definition to the social rate of discount, following the formulation originally proposed by W. J. Baumol.

In a 1968 article, Baumol pointed out the difficulties of an exact operational definition.[3] Government taxation of corporations, in order to be efficient, must provide more social benefits than if the funds paid as taxes had been left with the corporation. At a 50 percent tax rate, "the transfer of our resources R has led to a reduction of outputs for which consumers would have been willing to pay enough to provide a rate of return of 2r on corporate capital."[4] In other words, if consumers are willing to purchase corporate stock yielding 8 percent over the long term, they would be willing to pay 16 percent for such stock if corporate earnings were not taxed.* This high rate of discount is modified because of several externalities where private risk is greater than social risk, warranting the use of higher discount rates for private ventures. First, an individual's project is much riskier for him than for society at large, which is "insured" by the law of large numbers to the extent there are many projects being undertaken simultaneously. Second, if the individual's project is taken away from him for financial or other reasons, the benefits from the project continue to accrue to society.

Baumol's conclusion is that a higher discount rate than the current interest rate on government bonds should be used for analyzing government investment projects. The average corporate taxless return rate (2r) may also be too high because of the externalities discussed above. Baumol believes that a rate somewhere between the corporate taxless return rate and a government bond rate, with his preference toward the higher end of the scale, is the best feasible formulation for the social rate of discount.[5]

---

*As will be shown in Chapter six, the shareholders' return on equity is the current dividend yield plus the percentage rate of growth of dividends.

5

A THEORY OF
INVESTMENT
INCENTIVES

INTRODUCTION

The purpose of chapter five is to provide an understanding of which incentives are more effective and possible improvements in the government program. Applications of these improvements to other developed countries will be considered.

The chapter will have four sections:

1. A study of the special benefits and costs of depressed area locations to the foreign investor.

2. A consideration of the various types and effectiveness of incentives that governments offer to investors.

3. A discussion of possible improvements in the types of subsidies available and the manner in which the amount of subsidy for a given project is decided.

4. A consideration of the extent to which conclusions reached regarding Belgian depressed areas might have broader applications to depressed area programs in other developed countries.

BENEFITS AND COSTS OF DEPRESSED
AREA LOCATIONS

The location of an investment in a depressed area with the benefit of an incentive entails certain marginal special costs that differ from those in a normal location. It is the purpose of this section to analyze these special costs.

It has already been seen that Belgium bases its primary depressed area subsidy on the fixed assets of the investment. Because the expenditure for fixed assets represents fixed costs from the point of view of the investor, these subsidy programs are streams of payments that lower the fixed costs to the investor.[1] The benefit of the investment incentives, like other fixed costs, has nothing to do with the actual amount of production once the expenditure for the plant and its equipment has been completed on the basis of expected demand.

The special costs that are associated with depressed area locations are likely to be of two types. The first of these is additional transport costs, both on inputs and finished products that are incurred because of the relatively unattractive, noncentral plant location.[2] These costs for a given amount of production will vary according to the industry. Transport-oriented industries are those in which there is typically a high bulk or weight to value-added component. This type of industry is usually either material or market oriented. Examples are food, petroleum, and chemicals—all industries that showed a fairly low propensity to invest in depressed areas in Belgium.[3]

The second type of special cost in depressed area plant locations is labor cost. In a static case it is possible in theory that lower wage rates in the depressed area are offset by even lower (relative to the national average) labor productivity.[4] This would result in higher per-unit costs in the depressed area location. This productivity problem is probably not an important consideration in Belgium where education and labor skills are relatively widespread and advances in educational levels appear not to have contributed very heavily to national growth.[5]

These two special cost factors, labor and transport marketing, are not unique to depressed areas. Their importance is that they represent the most sizeable marginal costs (transport and marketing) or marginal savings (labor) of a depressed area location relative to normal areas. Both labor and transport costs are variable costs, whereas the subsidy, being based on fixed assets, is a reduction in fixed costs.

The net effect of the depressed location will depend on the benefits conferred by that location relative to its costs.* The variable

---

*This may be expressed in mathematical terms from the company's point of view of the present value of benefits and costs associated with a depressed area location as

$$NB = \sum_{n=1}^{\infty} \frac{b_n + qn\,(W_n - W_n\,^*) - T_n\,(K_n - K_n\,^*)}{(1 + r)n}$$

costs associated with depressed area locations may outweigh the
variable benefits for two reasons. First, there are more material-
or market-oriented industries than there are labor-oriented industries
in a developed country.[6] This means that in most cases of the multinational firms locating in a depressed area the total net variable
costs associated with a depressed area location will be higher as
compared with a location in another region. Second, even for those
industries that are labor oriented, there are social and technological
factors that limit the benefit conferred by extremely low wages. The
existence of national minimum wage laws often keeps the wage rate
in depressed areas above the level it would be without government
intervention in the factor markets.[7] The existence of minimum wage
laws may limit the per unit benefit (W_n -W_n *) that the firm gains
from location in depressed areas because the W_n* is kept artificially
close to the national wage level. Also, it appears that the labor-
capital ratio is quite uniform for foreign investment because these
firms prefer to utilize similar technological methods throughout the
world.[8] This level of technology utilized may tend to fix the labor-
capital ratio and limit the substitution of increased quantities of
cheaper labor in the depressed area.

The conclusion to this discussion of the benefits and costs of
depressed area locations on the foreign investor is that the special
costs of depressed area locations probably outweigh the special
benefits in most cases. This conclusion is hardly surprising because
any other conclusion would deny the existence of depressed areas
caused by a lack of industrial growth in the region.

----

where   NB = present value of net benefit of location in depressed
                areas
        b = The sum of all subsidies paid by the government
        q = the quantity of labor hired per period
        W = the average national wage paid by an industry in which
                the foreign investor is a member
        W* =the average actual (or expected) wage paid by the foreign
                firm in the depressed area
        T = average annual number of units transported
        K = the average per unit transport and marketing costs that
                would have been paid by the firm in a nondepressed
                area location that would have minimized this cost
        K* = the actual (or expected) per unit transport and marketing
                costs paid by the firm in the depressed area
        n = time periods over which the net benefit is to be calculated
        r = the company's cost of capital.

The role of the investment incentive in this process is to compensate for the marginal special costs of a depressed area location. As has been shown, the calculation of the net benefit to the investor should include the amount of the subsidy as well as the marginal special costs and benefits of the depressed area location. Ideally, the subsidy should be the factor making the depressed area location attractive by providing a marginally larger amount of inducement than the disincentive provided by an excess of special costs of the depressed area location over special benefits. This implies that when the special costs (transport and marketing) are less than the special benefits (labor) then there should be no subsidy paid.

TYPES AND EFFECTIVENESS OF VARIOUS INCENTIVES

The types of incentives offered by developed countries to foreign investors may be divided into two main groups. The first group is composed of that type of incentive that is not a use of funds from the point of view of the host government. This type of incentive usually involves the government's foregoing future receipt of payments from the foreign investor that, in the normal course of business, have to be made. Examples of non-fund-using incentives are those such as exemptions from income taxes, special provision for accelerated depreciation allowances, government guarantees to credit institutions to obtain financial assistance for the foreign investor, and others.

The second group of incentives are fund-using incentives from the government's standpoint because they involve real transfer payments between the government and the foreign investor. Examples of these types are the direct capital grants, which most countries regard as their most important incentive in regional development programs, and interest rate subsidy programs that are utilized in Belgium.

Non-Fund-Using Incentives

In general, non-fund-using incentives are of minor importance as incentives to promote regional development in developed countries. Their minor position is a result of legal systems in the capital exporting countries that limit their effectiveness for the foreign investor.

The incentive that has nominally the greatest importance is that of a reduction or exemption from the income taxes of the host country. This incentive is limited because most capital-exporting developed countries have legal systems that attempt to avoid

imposing double taxation on its foreign investment abroad.[9] For
example, U.S. tax law allows a derivative tax credit resulting from
foreign tax payments to be credited against the amount of U.S. tax
that would normally be paid on the amount of dividends repatriated to
the U.S.[10] This means that for an American investment benefiting
from total tax exemption that earns $100 profit in country X, its
payment to country X would be zero. If it is further assumed that
the U.S. tax rate is 50 percent and that of country X is 40 percent,
then the total forgone by country X is $40 (40 percent of $100). The
company in this case has a total U.S. tax burden of $50 (50 percent
of the total profit of $100). Assuming all subsidiary profits are to
be remitted to the U.S. parent in the form of dividends, the company
without the tax holiday would normally have had to pay $40 to the host
government and $10 to the U.S. government, so that the net total
benefit provided by the tax exemption to the company is zero.[11] The
zero effective benefit to the company is therefore much lower than
the cost forgone by the government. From the point of view of the
foreign investors this type of incentive is, of course, not an incentive
at all because it provides no net benefit for developed country location.[12]

There is divided opinion whether accelerated depreciation and
other capital consumption allowances are an inducement to invest.[13]
Most developed countries have provision for accelerated depreciation
allowances, and some allow higher than the normal rate for depressed
area investments. For example, the United States allows 78 percent
of the asset value of plant and machinery to be depreciated within a
five-year period (including the effects of the 7 percent investment
credit).[14] Comparable figures for other major developed countries
are Belgium, 92 percent; Canada, 71 percent; France, 76 percent;
West Germany, 67 percent; Italy, 100 percent; Japan, 68 percent;
the Netherlands, 86 percent; Sweden, 100 percent; and the United
Kingdom, 91 percent.[15] The problem with accelerated depreciation
from the viewpoint of the foreign investor is that the legal systems
of most developed countries and the accounting systems most often
used by multinational firms have combined a limit the effectiveness
of this as an incentive.

Unlike the United States, many developed countries follow the
pattern of Belgium in requiring that the same system of depreciation
be used for tax and public financial purposes. In the United States
corporations can utilize accelerated depreciation for the tax book,
limiting their tax liability, and then use straight-line depreciation
for the published financial statements, allowing them to show higher
profits. In the other developed countries the use of accelerated
depreciation lowers the taxable income by the amount of the extra
depreciation, but similarly lowers the firm's local profits as well.[16]

Accelerated depreciation allowances are an incentive in that their use permits deferring taxes into the future that would normally have been paid earlier using normal depreciation procedures. The yearly amount of depreciation tax savings is equal to the annual amount of depreciation on the new investment times the corporate tax rate.[17] The annual incentive from the use of accelerated depreciation is the tax savings using accelerated depreciation less the tax savings from the use of normal depreciation.

The use of accelerated depreciation does not reduce total tax payments, but it does push them further into the future. Thus the value of accelerated depreciation to the foreign investor largely depends on the investment gains he can realize from the funds he has "borrowed from the taxman" at an interest-free rate.*

In addition to affecting profits, accelerated depreciation allowances are by their nature very different than investment incentives.[18] Depreciation reform is a means for the more accurate charging of the actual amount of capital consumed to current production costs. Changes in depreciation methods, by their nature, tend to be general in effect upon the entire economy. Investment incentives, on the other hand, are especially aimed at certain regions or types of investment and are much more specific in nature. The attempt to use a general instrument to accomplish a specific purpose may create more negative aspects than would the use of a less general instrument.[19]

In conclusion, it is apparent that favorable depreciation allowances do not provide large profit incentives to the foreign investor and that they cannot easily be used as the primary investment incentives in a regional development program.

The third non-fund-using type of incentive offered by host governments to attract investment to depressed areas is the giving of government guarantees to credit institutions as an aid in obtaining credit. The value of this is obvious, particularly in periods of tight money. However, in practice the advantage is apt to be more attractive to the small firm wishing to locate in the depressed area inasmuch as the large multinational firm, by virtue of its size and cash flow, is able to obtain credit in almost all situations. This special access to capital was one of the special advantages listed by Kindleberger in his discussion of the form and nature of the international investor.[20] It is doubtful, given this fact, whether the guarantee of the host government in order to facilitate the giving of credit to the foreign investor

---

*For those who find this explanation unclear, the technical aspects of accelerated depreciation allowances are explained, using examples, in Chapter 6.

can ever be a predominantly determining factor in the location decision of a larger foreign firm in a developed country. For the smaller firms, the credit guarantee could be a significantly more important factor.

Fund-Using Incentives

As has already been seen, fund-using incentives are the primary type of incentive given to induce investment in depressed areas of developed countries. There are two basic types of fund-using incentives that have found widespread acceptance. These are the interest rate subsidy, such as is found in Belgium, and the direct capital grant, such as is widely used by other developed countries and is available in Belgium as an alternative to the interest rate subsidy.

The interest rate subsidy, based on fixed assets investment, is the primary form of incentive in Belgium and is also widely used in the Netherlands and Luxembourg.[21] It has the same effect as does the direct capital grant of lowering the effective cost of the fixed assets. The payment of a tax-free subsidy (s) to a foreign investor involves the loss of the entire (s) to the host government. The benefit (b) to the company is not equal to the entire amount of the subsidy, because in Belgium, as in the United States, interest expense is a tax deductible expense. (b) is equal to the amount of subsidy received times the percent of the total subsidy that was not tax deductible.* However, the cost of the subsidy to the government is counterbalanced by its collecting higher taxes over the life of the loan. This arises from lower tax deductions of the company than if it had borrowed money at market rates and deducted the interest expense.

---

*In mathematical notation,

$$b = s\ (1-t)$$

where b = benefit to the company that is tax-deductible
s = amount of subsidy paid by the government
t = effective tax rate.

For a simple numerical example, take the set of figures of a highly desirable investment in a 1966 depressed area in Belgium as presented in Table 8, page 26. In this example, the government subsidized the interest expense to the amount of BF 27.1 million. If the company had paid the entire interest expense the tax deductible nature of that expense (at a 35 percent tax rate) would reduce the benefit to the company to BF 17.6 million.

The net cost of the subsidy may be defined as the subsidy amount less the present value of taxes that would not have been collected with full interest tax deductions. It is clear to the extent that the subsidized industries have low profit, low growth labor-intensive characteristics of the depressed area investment studied in 1967-68 and that the expected net cost to the government will be higher than with more profitable industries. There is a risk that any given investment might not be profitable. If there are no profits then there are no future tax revenues from the reduction of interest expense to offset the gross cost to the subsidy. Assuming there is a greater probability that an investment in a high-profit industry will be more profitable than another investment in a low-profit industry, then the expected net cost of the subsidy to the government will be higher for the low-profit industry investment, because of the greater risk that this investment might not generate future taxable profits.

In summation, the benefit of the interest subsidy to the company is the difference between the after-tax subsidized interest rate and the after-tax market interest rate. The net cost of the subsidy to the government is the gross amount of the subsidy less the expected present value of taxes paid by the investor on revenues that would have been shielded from taxes by full interest expense deductions. The net cost of the incentive partially depends on the future tax inflows, which in turn depend on the future profitability of the investment.

The tax-free direct capital grant is an alternate form of subsidy available to investors in Belgium. From the point of view of the investor the direct grant has two important advantages over the interest rate subsidy. The first is that the entire amount of the subsidy is payable initially instead of being spread over the five-year period of the interest subsidy. For example, let us take the case of an investment of BF 150 million that receives the maximum subsidies. The base amount on which the subsidy is calculated in two thirds of the investment, or BF 100 million in this example.[22] As seen from Table 8, assuming a 9 percent market interest rate the subsidy paid by the government would be a total of BF 27.6 million—BF 9.0 million in year 1, BF 8.1 million in year 2, BF 4.0 million in year 3, BF 3.5 million in year 4, and BF 3.0 million in year 5. According to capital budgeting theory, the subsidy's value to the company is the present value at the time the investment decision is made at the company's cost of capital on a after-tax basis.[23] If this subsidy stream of payments is converted to an after-tax cost to express its true benefit to the company and present valued at 10 percent (the assumed cost of capital to the company) the net benefit in year 1 of the stream of subsidy is BF 14.5 million.

The entire amount of the direct capital grant formerly could be obtained in year 1 instead of being spread over five years. The value of a grant thus obtained is BF 18.0 million (equals the total subsidy of BF 27.1 million x .65 to convert to an after-tax basis) implying a present value advantage of BF 3.5 million in favor of the capital grant. However the Belgian Authorities have indicated that the capital grant is now paid with the same timing as the subsidized loan.

The direct capital grant has a second advantage over the interest rate subsidy. The grant is a nondebt source of funds that does not constitute a marginal use of existing debt capacity as expressed in conventional debt-equity ratios, while the subsidized loan is a use of such debt capacity. The grant has advantages for corporate financial reasons over the interest rate subsidy.[24]

Despite the economic advantages of the direct capital grant, most foreign investment in Belgium has preferred the interest rate subsidy. This has ocurred for two primary reasons. First, the demand for local borrowing has been largely due to the impact of U.S. direct investment controls. The Foreign Direct Investments Regulations of the U.S. government set investment limits for companies in Europe. The retained earnings and any debt or equity outflow from the U.S. parent to the European subsidiary are considered increases in foreign direct investment, while foreign borrowing is considered a reduction. In order to stay within their quotas, U.S. companies are forced to borrow abroad. Given this need for foreign borrowing, subsidized loans in Belgium have been extremely attractive.[25] Second, there has been a lack of clarity in government explanations of the subsidy system. Government representatives emphasize that if a company needs debt financing it is better to take the interest rate subsidy, and if the company does not need local debt the direct capital grant is preferable. Since many American corporations are under pressure because of their investment quotas, they decide on the interest rate subsidy. However, these two alternatives are not mutually exclusive. It is possible to arrange local financing through the government at full market interest rates and obtain the direct capital grant with its present value advantage and corporate finance advantages. This combination of government sponsored loans at market rates and capital grants had not occurred to either of the two government spokesmen interviewed by the author and to their knowledge has not been utilized by any foreign investor.[26]

Variable cost subsidies do not exist in Belgium, but should be considered in the list of possible effective investment incentives.

It was illustrated in the section entitled "Benefits and costs of Depressed Area Locations" of this chapter that the inherent costs of a depressed area location to the foreign investor tend to take the form of higher variable costs. It was also shown that one of the primary goals of the Belgian government was to increase employment in its depressed areas. This increase in employment in the depressed region is, from the point of the foreign investor, an increase in variable costs. If the host government goal is to increase one component of variable costs (employment), and if the inherent nature of depressed area location tends to increase other variable costs factors (transport and marketing costs), it is illogical that the government should attempt to subsidize this investment by reducing the effective cost of fixed assets. A much more effective method might be to subsidize labor costs directly.

The first developed country that has utilized this approach to regional development subsidy programs is Canada. The Canadian government, in its Regional Development Incentives Act of 1969, provides for the one-shot payment of $5,000 per new worker employed in a designated region.[27] The Minister for Regional Economic Expansion, Jean Marchand, emphasized in his speech before the passage of the Incentives Act that the incentives are to be given on strictly a one-shot basis.[28] The vast majority (80 percent) of the incentive is payable when the investment "has been brought into commercial production."[29] The remainder of the incentive is payable over a period not to exceed forty-two months after the date of payment of the first 80 percent of the subsidy.[30]

The Canadian Incentives Act seems to be a good new approach to investment incentives in developed countries, given the nature of the marginal benefits and costs of depressed area locations.

EXTENSIONS AND IMPROVEMENTS IN THE BELGIAN REGIONAL DEVELOPMENT PROGRAM

A primary criticism that can be made of the formulation of the regional development program is the government's lack of basic industry cost information upon which to base the subsidies. As has been observed, the purpose of the Belgian depressed areas program is to provide an effective inducement at the margin to compensate an investor for the special costs inherent with most industries located in a depressed area. The problem is that cost conditions vary exceedingly from industry to industry. It is very possible that for a labor-intensive industry such as textiles, the special benefits of depressed area location (low wage rates) would outweigh the special costs of such a location (transport and marketing costs). In this situation a subsidy is not needed to compensate the investor for locating in what is for him the most favorable cost location, even though this location is in a depressed area. It is equally possible

that for a highly transport-oriented industry (petroleum refining)
there is no subsidy available under the program that will marginally
compensate for the additional transport costs of a depressed area
location. The adequacy of a subsidy to a given investment should be
judged relative only to the special cost factors of that industry.

The Belgian program studied in the 1967-68 period was
exclusively location oriented in that the size of the subsidy was
determined by the location of the investment. Most investments
locating in depressed areas received the maximum subsidy despite
the very real variances in cost conditions between industries. This
implies that the program tended to provide too large a subsidy for
those industries in which the marginal special benefits of depressed
area location approximated the marginal special costs of that location.
The author's opinion is that the government could have paid a smaller
subsidy to industries whose marginal special depressed area costs
are lower without material effects on the volume of foreign investment
going into the depressed areas.

In the absence of cost data it is difficult to prove that the government has been paying larger than necessary subsidies to certain
industries because of the relatively inflexible operation of the incentive plan. However, a World Bank recommendation in a similar
situation in Singapore corresponds to the author's observations about
Belgium. A World Bank team recently decided that Singapore was
paying larger than necessary subsidies to certain types of foreign
investment and recommended a reduction in the incentive levels.
The logic of the World Bank was that where there is a strong investment demand combined with a high level of subsidy use from certain
types of foreign investment, the investment demand function of these
industries is probably relatively inelastic. This implies that the
level of subsidies can be reduced for these industries without
materially lowering their volume of foreign investment.[31] Following
the logic of the World Bank team and looking at the high correlation
between the labor intensiveness of various industries studied in
Belgium and their tendency to invest in depressed areas, it is possible
to conclude that much of the labor intensive industry would have still
located in depressed areas even with a smaller subsidy.*

A corollary of this reasoning is that if total government
resources for the subsidy program are fixed and that less of this

---

*In Table 15 of this book the coefficient of determination (r^2)
between the industries tendency to invest in depressed areas and
labor intensiveness was .04. However, this is one coefficient that
was skewed because of the aggregation of industries. If the paper
and glass industry is omitted from the calculation, the r^2 becomes
.36.

total is allocated to labor intensive industries, then a larger residual amount will be available to encourage nonlabor-intensive industries into depressed areas.

A better data base of cost compositions of the industries would also help to select the most effective type of incentive to the investor. If average cost curves of the investor are expected to be flat for most reasonable production levels and the fixed cost component of total costs is also expected to be flat, then a subsidy based on fixed assets (a reduction of fixed costs) is an effective method of subsidy. This type of subsidy could be either the interest rate subsidy calculated on a fixed assets base or the direct capital grant calculated on the same base. With relatively flat cost curves, the subsidy based on fixed assets provides a constant inducement to increase production, because at any production level the subsidy is a constant percentage of total costs. In terms of marginal analysis, assuming flat average and average fixed cost curves and a subsidy based on fixed assets, the management of the plant knows that for the cost of each marginal unit a constant amount is being financed by the subsidy.

If the cost curves for the industry in question are believed to resemble textbook cost curves, then the subsidy to fixed assets might not be as effective for the marginal unit. As average costs increase beyond capacity, average fixed costs account for a steadily smaller portion of average cost. This implies that the fixed assets subsidy, by reducing average fixed costs, provides a smaller incentive for each marginal unit. On the other hand, an incentive based on variable costs, such as the Canadian subsidy per employee or a subsidy per unit produced above a base level, would provide an increasing inducement to continue production at higher levels.

In conclusion, it is important that the government has a reasonable idea as to the cost conditions in the various industries it is most likely to subsidize. This knowledge of cost conditions is important both in determining an optimal subsidy amount that will compensate the investor on the margin for the special costs of depressed area locations and in determining the form of the incentive. While cost curves for most industries are probably relatively flat over expected production levels, it is theoretically possible that for an industry with textbook-like cost curves the traditional subsidy to fixed costs could not be as effective as a subsidy to variable costs. Here the shape of the cost curves could have an effect on the form the subsidy takes.

Another conclusion is that it is a mistake to fix the level of subsidization at a relatively constant rate. Flexibility is important both in the amount of incentives given and the areas over which they are given. The need for flexibility is apparent if the subsidy is viewed as compensatory to the investor for the special costs of a depressed

area location, which as has been seen, vary widely from industry to
industry. To be effective to all types of industry the subsidy must
also be free to vary with these special costs.

Flexibility in the size of the subsidy also implies a greater
negotiating procedure with the foreign investor than if subsidies are
relatively fixed and automatic in amount. During this negotiation
period it should be possible to gauge from the investor's reaction to
various subsidy proposals the degree to which the subsidy compensates
that investor for his perceived marginal special costs of a depressed
area location. This negotiating procedure provides feedback with
which to update and reassess industry cost conditions.

In summation, the author's opinion is that increased flexibility
in both the amount and form of the subsidies would go a long way to
promoting the high-profit, high-value-added, high-growth industry
that was not attracted to Belgian depressed areas in 1967-68.

APPLICATIONS TO OTHER DEVELOPED COUNTRIES

The question to be answered in this section is how may the
conclusions concerning Belgium be applied to other developed countries.
The similarities and differences between depressed area programs
of Belgium and other developed countries will be examined before
briefly discussing the applicability of the Belgian case.

The first similarity is that there appears to be a relative
uniformity of the economic characteristics of subsidized firms locating
in depressed areas. There has been little empirical research in
this area, but the work that has been done seems to confirm the evidence
presented in the case of Belgium. The first evidence is taken from
the distribution of American foreign investment in Belgium in
1957-61 in response to the 1958 Regional Development Laws.[32] The
least profitable industries had a greater tendency to invest in
depressed areas in this period—a tendency that was similar to that
observed in 1967-68 with respect to the 1966 development areas.*
Ronald B. Gold has corroborated the fact that subsidies in Pennsylvania
tend to have a much greater effect on small industrial firms than they
do on larger ones.[33] He cites a survey of new investment in
Pennsylvania in which 89 percent of the small firms surveyed replied
that the subsidy was a vital influencing factor on their location
decision. In the same survey, responses from larger firms indicated
that only 21 percent of these regarded the subsidy as an important
locational factor.[34] Sar Levitan has accused the Area Redevelopment

---

*See pages 44-46 of this book.

Agency of subsidizing inefficient investment locations in its regional development program.[35] Other studies have agreed with the earlier conclusions of this study concerning the nature and effectiveness of various subsidies relative to the marginal costs of depressed area locations.[36]

The second similarity common to most developed countries is the existence of formally recognized depressed areas.* The fact that these areas are recognized implies that the governments have found programs to alleviate the regional economic distress.[37]

An additional similarity is a high degree of uniformity in the aims of the depressed area programs. These aims are typically those of increasing regional employment, reducing differences in regional incomes, and improving the industrial structure of the region. For example, in Canada the emphasis is on the creation of new jobs in slow-growth regional areas.[38] For Britain the regional development program is also aimed at increasing employment in the designated Development Areas and strengthening the regional industrial structure.[39] In Italy the development problems of the Mezzogiorno have led to a massive regional incentive program whose aim, again, is the alleviation of excessive unemployment in that area.[40] The important point is that there are regional development programs in most of the developed countries and that the aims of these programs and the primary tools—the incentives—to accomplish the aims are broadly similar. Certain specific differences between the most important subsidy measures in Belgium and the other developed countries will be discussed later in this section.

The first major difference between Belgium and other developed countries has to do with a number of economic and geographic factors that determine that country's attractiveness as a prospective site for foreign investment. These factors—market size, geographic area, and rate of growth of the economy—have all been advanced as important considerations in the location of foreign investment and they vary widely from country to country.[41] The conclusion here is that while the economic characteristics of the industries that most respond to subsidies seem to be similar in the developed world, the wider geographic and economic setting for these investments differ greatly.

A second major difference between Belgium and some other developed countries is the degree to which the central government

---

*In Australia, there is no formally recognized program on the federal level, although the states have individual programs. This information is the result of a visit to the Australian Consulate in New York City by the author.

controls the primary regional incentive programs. There has been
a trend throughout the developed world toward increased regional or
local control of incentive programs. In general, the central governments of Western Europe have tended to retain preponderant power
in this area, while outside of Europe the situation has been less
clear, with the central government holding varying degrees of power
over incentive programs.[42] In Canada the federal government has
a very thorough plan of incentives for regional development, but the
two wealthiest provinces—Ontario and Quebec—have also advertised
extensive incentive programs.[43] The best example of a noncentral
government program is in Australia, where the federal government
offers no incentives to foreign investment and each state has its own
program, with higher incentives being offered to foreign investments
in the rural areas.[44] For most of the developed world the control of
incentive programs for regional development still lies in the hands
of the central government. Because of this fact, the remainder of
this study will be concerned with incentive programs controlled by
the central governments.

A third important difference between Belgium and other developed
countries is in the specific type of incentives offered. Most developed
countries have geographically delimited depressed areas in which
high rates of subsidy are offered to prospective investors. This is
the case for the developed countries examined by the author—
Australia, Italy, France, Belgium, Canada, Germany, the United
States, and the United Kingdom (see Table 20 for specific subsidies
for depressed regions). Although all of the countries studied had
specific delimited areas, there is a great variation in the effective
rate of subsidy offered to the foreign investor. The maximum rates
of 25 percent of initial costs are offered by both France and Canada.
In addition, the Canadian subsidy for employment created can raise
the total subsidy to 50 percent of the investment cost of the project
(see Table 20).

In almost all countries there is preference for the direct
capital grant as the primary form of incentive. The major exception
is Belgium, where the interest rate subsidy is the most common
method, but it will be recalled that the investor can choose between
a capital grant of the same amount as the interest rate subsidy should
he so decide. In the developed countries studied there is an almost
general preference for incentives based on the amount of fixed assets
or capital costs of the investment. Table 20 illustrates the type
and maximum rate of incentives recently being offered to investors
in depressed areas.

One final difference between Belgium and the other developed
countries is the method used to designate depressed areas. In the
Belgian case the 1966 Law created only one level of depressed area.

TABLE 20

Selected Examples of Subsidies Available for Plant
Locations in Depressed Areas

Country	Primary Type Of Subsidy	Maximum Amount of Subsidy
Canada	Capital grants	The maximum subsidy is up to 25 percent of approved capital costs (Machinery, equipment, buildings) plus up to $5,000 per job created. Maximum limits are $12,000,000 or $30,000 per job created, whichever is the lower. Within these limits, the Canadian Government will provide up to one-half of the capital in a new project.
U.K.	Capital grants	The maximum subsidy is up to 22 percent of capital expenditures on plant, machinery and equipment. "Free Depreciation" allows machinery and equipment to be entirely written off for tax purposes in one year. An unusual additional benefit allows the investor to depreciate 100 percent of the cost of assets including the 22 percent paid by the grant.
France	Capital grants	The maximum subsidy is up to 25 percent of the costs of land, plant, equipment and machinery for new investments Extensions of existing facilities are limited to 20 percent The grant may not exceed $2,500 for job created in a new investment and $1,375 per job created while expanding and existing investment.
Italy	Capital grants and low interest loans	The capital grant is up to 20 percent of the amount of fixed assets. The long term loan is based on the amount of fixed assets as well and is available at interest rates as low as 4 percent.
Belgium	Low interest loans and capital grants	The subsidized loans are for up to 10 years based on 75 percent of the investment in fixed assets. The interest subsidy is up to 7 percentage points off market interest rates for five years with the second five years at market rates. The capital grant is calculated on the basis of a theoretical ten term loan on 75 percent of the investment in fixed assets. The amount of the grant is equal to the interest subsidy amount that would have been paid if the investor had selected the low interest loan.

Sources: Fur Canada, "Doing Business in Canada—Federal Incentives to Industry," Department of Industry, Trade, and Commerce (Ottawa 1970). For the U.K., "Incentives for Industrial Firms Setting Up in Britain," British Trade Development Office (New York, 1972). For France, "Investment Incentives in France," French Industrial Development Agency (Paris, 1971). For Italy, Banca Commerciale Italiana, Vade-Mecum for Foreign Investors in Italy (Milan, 1968). For Belgium, "Promotion of Foreign Investments in Belgium," Belgian Ministry of Economic Affairs (Brussels, 1971).

In theory the incentives could be adjusted according to the desirability
of the prospective investment, although in fact, as was seen, the
subsidies tended to become fixed. This approach of only one class of
depressed area is found in most other developed countries.* The
primary exception is France, where planners have divided their
depressed areas into three classes and alloted each category a rate
of subsidy commensurate with the degree of underdevelopment. This
is a case where there is considerable differentiation of depressed
areas; but here again within each category the rate of subsidy remains
relatively uniform regardless of the nature of the investment.[45]

The first conclusion is that while the main geographic and economic factors vary widely among the developed countries, there
appears to be a remarkable similarity in the economic characteristics
of the industries that tend to be influenced by incentives in their
locational decisions. Second, most of the developed countries studied
have depressed areas and depressed area programs. Furthermore,
the aims of these programs and the methods used to accomplish these
aims are remarkably similar in this sample of the major developed
countries. Third, while there was surprising uniformity among the
developed countries concerning the type of incentives given and the
methods behind the delimitation of the specific depressed areas,
there was a wide range in the effective rates of subsidy that were
offered.

This brief summary has shown that the aims of depressed area
programs, their methods (types of incentives offered), and their
results (types of industry attracted) appear to be quite similar in
most developed countries and correspond to the Belgian case. The
primary differences between developed countries related to geographic
and market size and the size of the subsidy available. The role of
the subsidy as compensatory to the investor for the marginal special
costs of depressed area location seems to be implicitly accepted
everywhere. However, as in Belgium, most countries appear not to
have gone the next step and inquired into the actual amount of the
special costs for various industries that the subsidy is designed to
offset. The common result of the few empirical studies cited earlier
is that, as in Belgium, the subsidy programs have primarily attracted
small, labor-intensive, low-profit types of industries. It is possible
that, as in Belgium, more efficient use of government resources
would result from basing incentives on actual marginal industrial
costs of depressed area locations, which in turn would require more
flexible subsidy programs. The extension of the Belgian study to

----

*It is the case for Belgium, Germany, and Canada. See the
sources cited for Table 20.

the "n" country case is clearly beyond the scope of this study. The
fragmentary evidence concerning depressed area programs in other
countries agrees with the author's primary observation and hypothesis
concerning Belgium.

6

HOW TO EVALUATE SUBSIDIES
IN SELECTING
A FOREIGN PLANT LOCATION

INTRODUCTION

There is an increasing tendency for host governments to offer a wide variety of subsidy measures to promote certain investment locations for foreign investment. In many cases these locations have proved less than optimal from the firm's point of view and on several occasions have resulted in sizeable losses. (For example, in 1968 the Raytheon Corporation was forced to write off its $28 million investment in the south of Italy.) The purpose of this chapter is to provide a method by which a firm can evaluate subsidies given for plant location. For purposes of clarity and simplicity, the discussion will be limited to subsidies given by developed country governments to promote investments in a depressed area. The method of analysis can, however, be modified for consideration of other types of subsidy measures in both developed and less developed countries. This chapter will discuss two primary issues. First, it will provide a method by which a break-even subsidy can be calculated. This break-even subsidy can then be compared to the actual subsidy offered to decide whether the subsidized plant location should be accepted or rejected. Second, it will summarize briefly the best method to calculate the subsidy component or true subsidy portion of the most prevalent available types of subsidies.

This chapter assumes familarity with present value and discounted cash flow methods. For a quick review of those areas, see H. Bierman Jr. and S. Smidt, The Capital Budgeting Decision (New York: Macmillan, 1971).

CALCULATING THE BREAK-EVEN SUBSIDY

Before considering the method by which a break-even subsidy may be calculated, we must first inquire why the subsidy is being given. In general, subsidies are given to promote investments in locations that would not normally be economically attractive. In this chapter the concern is specifically with subsidies given for a depressed area plant location, and it is therefore necessary that the marginal benefits and costs of this type of location are discussed briefly.

As has been seen, the marginal costs that are associated with a depressed area location are likely to be of two types. The first is additional transport costs on factor inputs and finished products that exist because of the relatively unattractive, noncentral locations of many depressed areas. These costs will be different in each industry. For example, petroleum, chemicals, and food are all transport-oriented industries with regard to plant location because of their high bulk or weight to value-added ratio.

The second type of marginal cost is labor cost. Because wage rates in depressed areas of a given country are generally lower than the national average, labor costs are usually a marginal savings to a foreign investor in deciding on a depressed area plant location.

These two special cost factors are of course not unique to depressed areas. Their importance is that they represent the most sizeable marginal costs (transport and marketing) or marginal savings (labor) for a plant location in a depressed area. The net effect of a depressed area location will depend on the benefits conferred by that location relative to its costs. The variable cost associated with depressed area locations may outweigh the variable benefits for two reasons. First, there are more material- or market-oriented industries than there are labor-oriented industries in a developed country. This means that, in most cases, for a multinational firm locating in a depressed area the total net variable costs associated with the depressed area location will be higher as compared with location in another region. Second, even for those industries that are labor oriented there are social and technological factors that limit the benefit conferred by low regional wages. The existence of national minimum wage laws often keeps the wage rate in depressed areas above the level it would be without government intervention in the factor markets. The existence of minimum wage laws limits the regional per-unit benefit that the firm gains by location in depressed areas because the regional wage is kept artificially close to the national wage level. It is also possible that the multinational firm's use of a similar worldwide technology may keep the labor-capital ratio quite uniform for a given firm throughout the developed world. Consequently, the level of technology utilized may tend to fix the labor capital ratio

TABLE 21

Example of Calculation of Break-Even Subsidy
(all figures in thousands of dollars)

	Years						
	1	2	3	4	5	6	7
Annual cash cost estimate for nonsubsidized location	1,600	1,625	1,650	1,675	1,700	1,725	1,750
Annual cash cost estimate in subsidized location	1,800	1,850	1,400	1,950	2,000	2,050	2,100
Net costs disadvantage of subsidized location	200	225	250	300	325	350	375

and limit the substitution of increased quantities of cheaper labor in
a depressed area.

It is concluded that, in general, the special costs of depressed
area locations outweigh the special benefits. This implies that annual
expected costs for an investment in a depressed area will normally
be higher than those for an alternative, equal sized investment in a
nondepressed area.

With this general understanding of the costs and benefits of a
depressed area location, we can now proceed to the calculation of the
break-even subsidy. This is done in two steps. First it is necessary
to forecast the expected cash flow costs for the least-cost depressed
area location. This forecast should be arrived at by utilizing the normal cost forecasting estimates common to all capital budgeting decision
methods. The preferable types of capital budgeting procedures are
those that incorporate risk analysis features which take into account
the degree of uncertainty in any capital budgeting procedure.[1] As
with all types of capital budgeting estimates where uncertainty is not
explicitly considered in deriving a "most likely" cost function, it is best
to test the sensitivity of the most important cost elements, particularly those such as transportation and labor costs, which are most
affected by a depressed area location. After estimating the cash out-
flows required for the best depressed area plant location, it is necessary to forecast, using the same methods, a cash flow cost function
for a best available investment location for which is no subsidy available.

8	9	10	11	12	13	14	15
1,775	1,800	1,825	1,850	1,875	1,900	1,925	1,950
2,150	2,200	2,250	2,300	2,350	2,400	2,450	2,500
400	425	450	475	500	500	525	550

Note: At the investor's 10 percent cost of capital, he requires a subsidy of more than $2,525,000 to accept a depressed area location. This break-even subsidy amount is calculated by taking the present value of the net cost disadvantage at a 10 percent rate.

This analysis assumes an identical investment in a subsidized and nonsubsidized location.

Using the cost functions estimated for the best subsidized and nonsubsidized locations we can proceed to the second step of the calculation of the break-even subsidy. This is done by subtracting the annual (or period) cash flow costs estimated for the subsidized location from those of the nonsubsidized location. The resulting figure is the annual (or period) net cash flow disadvantage of the subsidized location.

The break-even subsidy is the present value of this net cash flow disadvantage, obtained by discounting the cash flow at the investing firm's cost of capital or hurdle rate for investment in the host country.[2] The concept of the cost of capital has been widely discussed in both practical and academic literature and a detailed discussion is beyond the scope of this chapter. The cost of capital is that return on an investment that will leave the firm's investors just as well off in terms of earnings per share as they were before the investment was undertaken. It is, therefore, equal to the weighted average cost of debt and equity capital.[3]

The present value of the net costs disadvantage is the break-even subsidy amount. If the host government offers a subsidy larger than this amount, then the subsidized plant location should be accepted. If the host government offers a subsidy amount smaller than this amount, then the subsidized location should be rejected. If the subsidy is just equal to the break-even amount calculated, the firm should be indifferent as to subsidized or nonsubsidized plant location.

An example may clarify this discussion. Suppose the investor has an investment horizon of 15 years and has estimated his cash outflow for a nonsubsidized location as being $1.6 million in year 1 of the investment, rising to $1.95 million in year 15. The investor has similarly forecast cash outflow of subsidized location as being $1.8 million in year 1, rising $2.5 million in year 15. The investor subtracts the expected cash outflow for a subsidized location from that of a nonsubsidized location to obtain the annual net cash flow disadvantage of a subsidized location. When the investor takes the present value of this net cost function at his 10 percent cost-of-capital rate, the break-even subsidy is calculated as being $2,525,000. This example is illustrated in Table 21.

Since the break-even subsidy is entirely dependent on the cost of capital rate and the cash cost estimates, and since these forecasts (particularly the cash cost forecast) are extremely uncertain, it is important, as mentioned earlier, that a probabilistic forecasting technique be used in order that the break-even subsidy will properly reflect uncertainty. Examples of some probabilistic forecasting techniques are risk analysis, sensitivity analysis, and the use of such Bayesian statistical methods as decision trees.[4]

CALCULATING THE ACTUAL SUBSIDY OFFERED

Having now calculated the break-even subsidy, the problem now becomes one of deciding whether the present value of the subsidy offered by the host government is greater or lesser than the break-even subsidy. This presents a problem because host governments offer a variety of incentive measures, which are not directly related to the break-even subsidy. As was shown in Chapter 5, the three primary types of incentives are low interest loans, direct capital grants, and accelerated depreciation allowances. In order to decide whether or not a subsidized location is attractive it is necessary to calculate the true subsidy offered or the subsidy component of each of these types of incentives.

Calculating the Subsidy Component of
Direct Capital Grants

Direct capital grants are widely used in much of the developed world and are the easiest types of subsidies to analyze. The subsidy component of a direct grant is the after-tax amount of the grant. If the grant is tax free, as is the case in Belgium, then the subsidy component of the grant is equal to the amount of the grant. For example, if France gives a lump sum grant of $3 million, which is taxed at a marginal tax rate of 40 percent, then the subsidy component of the grant is $1.8 million.

If the grant is given over a period of years, the total subsidy component of the grant is the present value of the yearly after-tax grant amounts at the company's cost of capital.

To modify the previous example, assume the $3 million grant taxed at 40 percent is paid out in annual installments of $1 million in each of the first three years of the project. The annual after-tax grant amounts are $600,000 ($1 million x .60), and the subsidy component of the grant is $2,486,900. This represents the present value of the annual after-tax grant amounts at the assumed 10 percent company cost of capital rate.

Calculating the Subsidy Component of
Low-Interest Loans

The subsidy component of a low-interest loan is the present value of the after-tax interest savings based on the difference between borrowing at market and subsidized interest rates. For example, assume a company is making an investment in Belgium and has a choice between a subsidized BF 100 million loan repayable in ten equal annual installments, with an interest subsidy of 9 percent in the first two years and 5 percent for the next three years and the identical loan in Belgian francs at a market interest rate of 9 percent. Also assume the company's tax rate is 35 percent. (Leave aside for the moment the possibility that the the company's lowest cost marginal borrowing source is in a currency other than Belgian francs.)

Under these assumptions the present value subsidy component of obtaining low-interest financing instead of borrowing at market rates is BF 14,392,000 or 14 percent of the principal amount of the loan. This is calculated by multiplying the after-tax interest savings from the subsidized interest rate times the amount of the loan outstanding in each period. The after-tax interest savings is derived by subtracting the after-tax interest cost of subsidized borrowing from the after-tax cost of borrowing at market rates. The present value subsidy component is obtained when annual after-tax interest savings are present valued at the company's cost of capital. This procedure is shown in Table 22.

TABLE 22

Calculation of Present Value Subsidy Component of Low Interest Loan

(1) Year	(2) Amount of Loan Outstanding (BF millions)	(3) After-Tax Subsidized Interest Rate (%)	(4) After-Tax Market Interest Rate (%)	(5) After-Tax Interest Savings* (4 - 3) (%)	(6) Annual After-Tax Interest Savings (2 x 5) (BF millions)
1	100	0	5.85	5.85	5.85
2	90	0	5.85	5.85	5.26
3	80	2.60	5.85	3.25	2.60
4	70	2.60	5.85	3.25	2.28
5	60	2.60	5.85	3.25	1.95

*The after-tax interest is equal to the before-tax interest rate times one minus the tax rate, or

$$i_a = i_b (1 - t)$$

where i_a = after-tax interest rate
i_b = before-tax interest rate
t = corporate tax rate.

The present value at 10 percent of the annual after-tax interest savings is BF 14,392,000 or $321,203 at the present dollar-Belgian franc central rate.

96

Comparing Borrowing Opportunities in
Different Currencies

The interest rate that is compared to the subsidized interest rate in order to derive the interest savings should be the company's cheapest source of marginal borrowing for a term equivalent to the subsidized financing. Since the company's marginal borrowing may be in a currency different from that offered in a subsidized loan, there is the problem of calculating true interest rates that reflect both interest expense and cost of a possible currency revaluation. This is done by calculating the discount cash flow rate, taking the loan principal amount (in dollars) as an outflow and principal and interest repayments as cash inflows (also in dollars). If the loan is not in dollars it is necessary to apply the expected future exchange rate between the dollar and the local currency borrowed in order to derive the dollar amount of principal and interest repayment at a future date.

The resulting discounted cash flow rate (the cost of borrowing including both interest and exchange factors) is the interest-revaluation cost of the loan.

For example, assume the American investor is offered a loan of BF 100 million at a 6 percent interest rate, with the principal amount to be repaid in five equal annual installments. Assume also that the investor believes the Belgian franc will revalue by 10 percent relative to the dollar in year 3 and will remain at that exchange rate in years 4 and 5 of the loan. This means that 10 percent more of the total of interest and principal repayments in years 3, 4, and 5 will have to be repaid, in dollars than would be the case if no future revaluation of the Belgian franc were assumed. Using these assumptions Table 23 can be created.

The discount cash flow rate (DCF) obtained from the total cash flow is the interest-revaluation cost of the loan. The DCF on the total cash flow in this example is 7.97 percent. While the interest cost of the loan is only 6 percent, the interest-revaluation cost, calculated by including the most likely assumptions concerning future exchange rates, raises the cost of the loan to 7.97 percent. The problem with this method is that it allows for only one estimate of interest-revaluation cost, which depends upon a highly uncertain forecast about future exchange rates. A better approach that incorporates the probablistic nature of currency forcasting is to calculate interest-revaluation loan costs for several cases, rank these cases by their subjective probabilities, and derive the weighted-average interest-revaluation cost.

For example, assume we are offered 6 percent Belgian franc financing for five years. By incorporating five exchange rate assumptions and evaluating these assumptions by their subjective

TABLE 23

Calculation of the Interest-Revaluation Cost
of a Foreign Currency Loan

Period	Amount Borrowed	Principal Amount Repaid Per Period	Interest At 6% Per Annum Per Period	Total of Principal and Interest Payments	Revalua-tion Cost Per Period	Total Cash Flow Per Period
0	(100.00)	—	—	—	—	(100.00)
1		20.00	6.00	26.00	—	26.00
2		20.00	4.80	24.80	—	24.80
3		20.00	3.60	23.60	2.36	25.96
4		20.00	2.40	22.40	2.24	24.64
5		20.00	1.20	21.20	2.12	23.32

probability, we can generate Table 24. The cases represent the
individual exchange rate assumptions. The loan interest rate is the
interest rate without including any exchange risk. The interest-
revaluation cost includes both interest and revaluation costs. The
probability of occurrences are our best estimates as to the likelihood
of each exchange rate assumption being correct.

In this case the weighted best estimate for interest-revaluation
cost for borrowing Belgian francs is 6.93 percent. This cost should
then be compared with the company's best alternative borrowing
opportunity in dollar terms for a similar loan with a maturity. If
this alternative is dollar denominated, then the subsidy component
can be calculated, as was previously described, by deriving the present
value of the annual after-tax interest savings favoring the subsidized
loan. If the best alternative is another foreign currency, then the
weighted average interest-revaluation cost for that loan should be
calculated. This weighted average should then be compared with the
weighted average interest-revaluation cost for Belgian franc borrowing,
deriving the present value of the annual after-tax interest savings of
the cheaper loan.

Calculating the Subsidy Component of
Accelerated Depreciation Allowances

The value of accelerated depreciation allowances is that their
use allows deferring tax payments that would have been paid if normal

TABLE 24

Weighted Average Calculation of
Interest-Revaluation Cost
Subsidized Loan

(1)	(2)	(3)	(4)	(5)
		Loan-		
	Loan Interest	Revaluation	Probability	Weighted Aver-
	Rate Cost	Cost	of	age Cost
Case No.	(%)	(%)	Occurrence	(3 x 4) (%)
1	6	6	.10	.60
2	6	6.5	.15	.98
3	6	6.75	.35	2.36
4	6	7.15	.25	1.79
5	6	7.97	.15	1.20
	Weighted average interest-revaluation cost			6.93

depreciation measures were in effect. In order to understand the value of accelerated depreciation allowances, it is first necessary to understand the tax consequences of depreciation. Depreciation, as a noncash expense, provides an annual tax savings equal to that year's depreciation times the applicable corporate tax rate.

The nature and calculation of the subsidy component of accelerated depreciation can be best described using an example. Assume that the host country will allow the American investor to depreciate 50 percent of his $10 million capital investment in each of the first two years and that normally the investor would write off the investment over five years using a straight-line method. Further assume that the corporate tax rate in the host country is 35 percent and that the investors cost of capital is 10 percent. Using this information, Table 25 can be created to calculate the subsidy component of the accelerated depreciation allowance.

The subsidy component of accelerated depreciation is $363,000. This is obtained by multiplying the incremental depreciation in each year times the corporate tax rate to derive the tax savings through depreciation. This annual tax savings is then present valued at the company's cost of capital rate to derive the subsidy component.

The basic nature of the gains from accelerated depreciation is shown by a comparison of columns 6 and 7 of Table 25. On an undiscounted basis (see column 6) there is no gain from accelerated depreciation, because the gains on years 1 and 2 are exactly counterbalanced by the tax losses in years 3, 4, and 5. The gains from accelerated

TABLE 25

Calculation of the Subsidy Component of Accelerated
Depreciation Allowances

(1)	(2) Amount of Acceler- ated Depre- ciation	(3) Amount of Normal Depre- ciation	(4) Incremental Annual Depre- ciation (2-3)	(5)	(6) Tax Savings ($ thou- sands)	(7) Present Value at 10 Percent ($ thou- sands)
Years	($ million)	($ million)	($ million)	Tax Rate	(4 x 5)	sands)
1	5.0	2.0	3.0	.35	1,050	954
2	5.0	2.0	3.0	.35	1,050	848
3	—	2.0	(2.0)	.35	(700)	(526)
4	—	2.0	(2.0)	.35	(700)	(478)
5	—	2.0	(2.0)	.35	(700)	(435)
Totals					0	363

depreciation are in "borrowing from the taxman" by postponing tax
payments that normally would have been made in early years until
later years.

It is clear that the attractiveness of using accelerated depreciation is increased with the use of a higher discount rate. Since the
use of a higher discount may be an indication of increased risk,
accelerated depreciation might be more of a inducement to the foreign
investor in higher risk countries with more uncertain political and
economic situations than in the stable developed countries of Western
Europe, where the lower investment risk might be reflected in a lower
discount rate. In addition, highly profitable and rapidly growing
companies with high costs of equity capital might favor accelerated
depreciation allowances over other incentive forms because the
company's high cost of capital would be translated into the use of
a high discount for investment project analysis.

DECIDING WHETHER OR NOT
TO ACCEPT THE SUBSIDY

The decision of whether or not to accept the subsidy should be
made by comparing the required break-even subsidy, calculated as
described on pages 92-95 with the subsidy component of the incentive
being offered, derived as described on pages 94-101. If the subsidy

component is less than the required break-even subsidy, then the incentive should be turned down and the plant location in the non-depressed area should be selected. On the other hand, if the subsidy component is greater than the required break-even subsidy, then the incentive should be accepted and the investment should be made in the depressed area.

CONCLUSION

This chapter has discussed the methods by which an investor should decide whether or not to select a subsidized depressed area location. This decision involves calculating the break-even subsidy amount required to make the depressed area location more attractive than the best possible nondepressed area location. Next, the actual subsidy being offered should be compared with break-even subsidy amount. This involves calculating the subsidy component—the true subsidy portion—of the government incentive. The calculation of the subsidy component was described for direct capital grants, low interest loans, and accelerated depreciation allowances. Finally, the subsidy component amount should be compared with the break-even subsidy amount to determine whether or not the subsidized depressed area location should be accepted.

CHAPTER

7

CONCLUSION

This study has made two primary contributions. The first is
the analysis of the Belgian depressed areas program, based on
empirical data measuring the reactions of foreign investment to this
program. The empirical basis of this study was not obtained from
official documentation and then regressed in several versions, as are
many economic studies. Instead, the data were, in a sense, created
by the author. The creation involved going over lists of the names
of all large investors in Belgium from 1967 through 1970, classifying
these investments by nationality, size of equity investment, and industry,
and then plotting each individual location on a map of Belgium. Using
this data, conclusions were drawn contrasting the aims and the achieve-
ments of the Regional Development Program that would not have been
possible using published data.

The conclusions drawn from the Belgian empirical data agree
with the fragmentary evidence available from other developed countries
concerning the industrial characteristics of industries that have high
tendencies toward depressed area locations. Despite the long history
of subsidy programs for poverty areas, there have been few, if any,
other studies that measure the industrial characteristics of industries
having high tendencies to invest in depressed regions. This statement
illustrates the paucity of empirical research in this area more than
it does the completeness of the statistical work performed in this
study. The empirical evidence is limited because the small sample
and the resulting necessity to aggregate the total sample into only
seven classes of industry detract from the confidence that can be
placed in the results. However, the correlation coefficients showing
the inverse relation between profit levels and growth in production
and the tendency to invest in depressed areas were high enough to
suggest some significant relationship.

Although the empirical testing was a primary aim, the study also sought to evaluate the results of the program relative to its aims, and demonstrated that it succeeded in diverting a larger share of total new foreign investment into depressed areas than had previously been the case. Furthermore, the program was successful in alleviating unemployment in certain depressed areas because of the tendency of labor intensive industry to invest in these areas. The program failed in attracting high profit, high growth types of foreign investment into depressed areas. It also failed to attract much new foreign investment to the depressed areas of the poorest provinces, while benefiting more the depressed areas in provinces of average or higher national income.

The second contribution of this study consists of suggested changes in the allocations of subsidies that could improve the results of the program. It was shown that the basic nature of the subsidy is to compensate the investor for accepting the marginal costs of a depressed area location. Because these costs vary widely between industries, a relatively fixed subsidy rate will tend to provide too large a subsidy to those industries whose special depressed area costs are small (labor intensive industries) and will not be an inducement to those industries whose marginal special costs of depressed area location are large (capital intensive, high profit, high growth industries). The primary suggested improvement is to base subsidies on the actual marginal depressed area cost of the investor, which also implies that the subsidies must be flexible between industries and between regions.

This change would not involve a departure from the existing legal framework of the Regional Development Program in Belgium. The problem was that in the 1967-68 period, the government's open arms attitude toward foreign investment resulted in a tendency toward relatively fixed rate subsidies. This was evidenced by a sort of "most favored nation" treatment of each new foreign investor, who, in effect, successfully argued that because company X received r rate of incentive for locating in depressed area A, then my company Y should also receive r rate of incentive for locating in depressed area B. This approach ignores both the different cost conditions present in depressed areas A and B and the variances in industrial cost conditions for companies X and Y.

The purpose of the subsidy is to compensate the foreign investor at the margin for the marginal costs of a depressed area location. These costs, of course, are different for each depressed area location and with each type of industry. An optimal subsidy will be based on the true disincentive of the depressed area location relative to a minimal cost alternative. Any subsidy program not based on this true disincentive probably will provide too large an incentive to some foreign investors and not large enough a subsidy to others.

The author's opinion is that the failures of the Belgian program largely may be explained by this lack of government flexibility in the allocation of subsidies. The discussion of the marginal costs and benefits of depressed area locations has shown that high profit, high growth industries, whose failure to invest in depressed areas constitutes one failure of the program, tend to be low labor intensive, with a high dependence on transport and marketing facility. For this type of industry the marginal costs of a depressed area location is higher than for other types of foreign investment and a relatively fixed rate subsidy would probably not attract this type of investment at the margin.

Similarly, it was shown that the marginal costs of a depressed area location in the poorest provinces is probably greater than it is in the more affluent. Given a relatively fixed rate subsidy, one would expect foreign investment to be more attracted to the depressed areas in more affluent provinces with lower marginal depressed area costs and to avoid depressed areas in the poorest provinces with their generally higher marginal costs.

In conclusion, the author believes that a successful subsidy program, to attract foreign investors to depressed areas, has three components:*

1. The host government is convinced of the necessity for a depressed area program and is willing to provide adequate financial assistance.

2. The incentives given by the government are the types that are attractive to foreign investment. Examples of these are direct capital grants and interest rate subsidies.

3. The rate of subsidy is flexible and is based on the true disincentive of a given depressed area location to a firm in a given industry. This implies a better knowledge of various regional and industry cost conditions than the Belgian government now has.

The Belgian Regional Development Program, created by the Law of July 14, 1966, had the first two of these ingredients but lacked the third. The result was only a partially successful program, whose failures constitute an important lesson in the need for government flexibility in dealing with private foreign investment. Just as costs vary in a market economy, reflecting the underlying supply and demand forces, so should subsidy programs for regional development, if they are to be fully effective, be flexible enough to compensate the investor at the margin for variances in costs because of a depressed area location.

---

*This assumes that the host country is an attractive location to foreign investors to begin with.

AN ECONOMETRIC STUDY OF
U.S. DIRECT INVESTMENT IN THE COMMON MARKET

This appendix has two purposes: (1) to formulate several single equation models to explain the book value of U.S. direct investment in the Common Market (EEC) and changes in those book values for the 1958-68 period using variables that have been omitted from previous research; and (2) to test the forecasting ability of the models developed by contrasting the predicted and actual book values in 1969 and 1970.

Previous research treating this problem concentrated on such explanatory factors as market size, rate of market growth, and tariff effects. For example, V.N. Bandera and J.T. White tested the period 1953-62 for the relation between the level of U.S. direct investment (as measured by the book value of U.S. firms in the EEC) with variables such as national income levels, changes in those levels, changes in international liquidity, and annual earnings.[1] They concluded that the absolute level of national income was the most significant factor. A.E. Scaperlanda and L.J. Mauer (referred to hereafter as S & M) tested the period 1952-66 and two component periods, 1952-58 and 1959-66, in order to determine the importance of a series of variables to annual change in book value of U.S. direct investment.[2] They tested such independent variables as the absolute level of gross national product in the EEC (selected as a proxy variable for market sizes), a variable selected to determine tariff distortion effect, and several proxy variables for changes in the rate of Common Market income. The results were very high $\bar{R}^2$ for most estimating equations, with particularly high levels of significance for the market size variable. The role of GNP level in the 1959-66 period was more important than it was in the 1952-59 period, confirming S & M's hypothesis that foreign investment was positively determined by market size as the EEC became a progressively more integrated market.

Although the previous empirical evidence pointing toward absolute level of market size as the determining factor in U.S. direct investment in the EEC, there are other plausible hypothesis concerning the motivation of this investment that have not been considered. The purpose of this appendix is to test other variables, which are briefly introduced below.

1. Profit, the traditional motive for foreign investment, is not
tested anywhere. S & M correctly point out that the level of return
on equity for U.S. corporations was lower in the Common Market
than in the United States for much of the period tested in their research. This is, in the author's belief, an overly simplistic analysis
because of the role of transfer pricing in the multinational corporation.
Although U.S. Commerce Department data on foreign investment is
presented in a highly aggregated form, one major industry, the petroleum industry, is broken out separately. In this industry, which con-
stituted 27.6 percent of the total book value of U.S. investment in the
EEC in 1970, transfer pricing operated to allocate taxable income
to producing rather than marketing ventures.[3]

2. There are a number of supply-related considerations that
have not been tested. The previous empirical research has been
done on the theory that foreign direct investment is induced mainly
by demand factors such as size and rate of growth of local markets
and local profit levels. However, there is some evidence to indicate
that supply factors may also play an important role.[4] The supply
factors considered here are wage differentials, U.S. corporate profits
(before tax), and an annual, average cost of capital rate for large
U.S. corporations.

Hypothesis Explanation and Model Formulation

The method employed in the testing of the explanatory variables
was that of OLS (ordinary least squares) linear multiple regression.
Various linear functional forms were tested and the normal linear
form was selected since it yielded the best preliminary results. The
regression strategy employed included the use of stepwise methods,
"forward selection" based on one or two variables and "backward
elimination" based on all or most of the explanatory variables.[5]
Various time lags were tested and, with minor exceptions, did not
improve the explanatory power of the equations. The lagged variable
that did improve the results most notably was that of U.S. corporate
profits before income taxes, lagged one year. Since we are interested
in determining both the absolute level of foreign investment and its
rate of change, two models were formulated.

$$I = f \ (Y, \ dY, \ P_{us}, \ w, \ T, \ P_{cm}, \ K)$$
$$dI = f \ (Y, \ dY, \ P_{us}, \ w, \ T, \ P_{cm}, \ K)$$

where:

I   = Annual dollar amount of book value of U.S. direct investment in the EEC[6]

dI   = Annual change in the dollar book value of U.S. direct
investment in the EEC[7]

Y   = Annual gross national product of the EEC at current
prices[8]

dY   = Annual dollar change in the GNP of the EEC at current
prices[9]

P_{us} = Annual dollar amount of U.S. corporate profit levels
before corporate income taxes[10]

w   = Ratio of average EEC hourly wages in manufacturing to
average hourly U.S. wages in manufacturing; the EEC figure is a
weighted average, with the national hourly wages weighted by each
EEC's country share of U.S. book value in the EEC[11]

T   = X/E

E   = Dollar value of annual exports from EEC countries to
other EEC countries[12]

X   = Dollar value of U.S. annual exports to the EEC[13]

P_{cm} = Annual dollar profit from U.S. direct investment in the
Common Market, restated to assume that all petroleum investment
earns an average petroleum industry return on equity as computed
from the various Fortune 500 annual calculations[14]

K   = Annual cost of capital for large U.S. companies.[15]

The importance of variable Y (market size) to the foreign
investor revolves around the principle of economies of scale. The
advantage of a large market is that a direct investor can achieve
low per-unit costs of production because the large market permits
the employment of advanced technology and the efficient specialization
of the factors of production. This is a familiar point in the literature
and does not need to be elaborated here.[16]

The reason for including increase in market size (variable dY)
as an explanatory variable to foreign investment is that a company's
opportunity for growth is normally related to market growth. Rapid
market growth means that an opportunity for rapid company growth
exists, which is itself an incentive to make the foreign investment.

U.S. corporate profit levels before income tax (P_{us}) was
selected because profitability is a primary constraint to both foreign
and domestic investment decisions. In addition to reducing internal
cash flow, low profitability reduces the availability and terms of new
equity financing by decreasing the price of a firm's stock. Lower
profits decrease the credit rating of a company and increase the
interest expense associated with new debt financing. Corporate
profits before tax were included because investments are tax deductible and are a superior measure of corporate profits available for
investment purposes.

Another explanatory variable is the wage differential ratio (w) for hourly workers in manufacturing between the EEC countries and the United States.[17] Jorgensen and Siebert tested a variety of hypothesis of the determinants of business investment and concluded the best hypothesis is that desired investment is proportional to the value of the output divided by the price of the factors of production.[18] Since the primary component of cost is wages, it is necessary to evaluate the importance of wage differentials to the foreign investment decision.

The increase in the EEC common external tariff is also widely held to be an important factor in inducing increased American investment to that area. Since trade and investment are substitutes, restrictions on the movement of one of these may lead to an increase of the other.[19] With regard to a common market, economic theory would indicate that the higher external tariffs could be expected to stimulate an inflow of investment from the outside. A proxy variable to measure this tariff distortion and investment stimulation effect is the variable T, taken from the S & M study.[20] T is a ratio of annual exports from the United States to the EEC divided by annual exports from EEC countries to other EEC countries. The theoretical expectation is that the higher external tariff should induce this ratio to decline over time, reflecting the export-creating nature of the Common Market for its partners and the export diversion for the rest of the world.[21] In the 1958-68 period covered by this study, the ratio in fact declined from .354 in 1958 to .212 in 1968. Although this ratio has weaknesses in that it does not address itself directly to the level of tariffs or attempt to account for any changes that would have occurred in the ratio if tariffs had remained constant, the author believes, as did S & M, that it is a reasonable proxy variable for tariff distortion effects.

The next explanatory variable to be considered is that of annual dollar profit from U.S. direct investment in the Common Market (P_{cm}). This is stated from U.S. Department of Commerce figures to include the assumption that all petroleum investment earns the same average return on book value that is earned by all large American integrated petroleum companies.[22] This restatement was done in order to remove the downward bias on book profits in marketing and other downstream ventures that result from the transfer pricing mechanism in the petroleum industry.[23]

The final explanatory variable to be considered is that of the cost of capital for large American corporations (K). Although the literature on the cost of capital is very complex, the author has attempted to calculate a cost of capital figure that at least directionally relates the level of EEC investment and the changes in that level to the perceived costs to American firms making the investment. The

cost of capital was calculated by taking the marginal cost of debt
and equity financing, weighted by the size of each component.[24] The
cost of debt financing was assumed to be equal to the average annual
bond rate as reported by Standard and Poor's multiplied by an
assumed 50 percent tax rate to arrive at an after-tax debt cost.[25]
The cost of equity financing was assumed to be the annual industrial
earnings per share divided by the annual average industrial price
per share, also quoted by Standard and Poor's and expressed in
percent. While acknowledging that this is not the best formulation,
it does have some theoretical justification and the added practical
advantage of being possible to calculate.[26] The rationale for calculating the cost of equity capital in this manner is that an investor
is paying a present value amount (the share price) for present and
expected future earnings. If present and and future earnings are
regarded as an annuity, then the percentage obtained by dividing the
earnings per share by share price is the discounted cash flow rate
that makes the future expected stream of earnings equal to today's
stock price.[27]

Empirical Results

Variables Affecting the Book Value of
U.S. Direct Investment

　　　Appendix Table 1 shows the results of stepwise and normal
OLS regression analysis for a single equation model with the book
value of U.S. direct investment in the EEC as the dependent variable.
The equations show very high $\bar{R}^2$, low standard errors of estimate
(relative to the magnitude of the dependent variable I), and varying
degrees of autocorrelation.

　　　In general, although the explanatory variable of income is the
most important, there are other variables not previously tested in
empirical research that are also important. For example, in equation
1.2, both the rate of increase of GNP and U.S. corporate profit levels
before income taxes are significant at the .05 level. In addition, the
wage differential variable is important, with a t-score significant at
the .12 level.

　　　This specific ordering of the explanatory variables by their
statistical importance is generally confirmed in all equations. The
level of GNP, its rate of change, the U.S. corporate profit level before
taxes, and the wage differential are more signficant than the other
variables of cost of capital in the U.S., profitability of U.S. firms in
the Common Market, and the tariff distortion effect wherever they
are tested. For example, in equation 1.5, which tests most of the

APPENDIX TABLE 1

Book Value of U.S. Direct Investment in the EEC
and Various Explanatory Variables

Equation	$\bar{R}^2$	SE	DW
1.1 I=-3424.38 + 32.376y (27.08)**	.9865	295.8	.632
1.2 I=-2344.71 + 33.17y -29.76dy +29.73P_{us} -8936.4w (8.60)**(-2.63)* (2.44)* (1.57)	.9939	181.8	2.22
1.3 I=-2683.13 +33.57y -29.84dy +26.83P_{us} -8760.56w (7.70)**(-2.44)* (1.68) (1.41) +73.35k (.33)	.9940	197.1	2.15
1.4 I=-1901.5 +32.58y +33.33P_{us} -13072.9w (6.22)**(2.02) (1.76)	.9906	247.1	1.91
1.5 I=-3127.35 +38.96y -27.02dy +35.11P_{us} (4.30)* (-2.03) (2.27) -12339.8w +1.55P_{cm} -2176.24T (1.59) (.57) (.61)	.9935	205.28	2.31
1.6 I=-3487.58 +26.24y +26.80P_{us} (6.17)** (1.50)	.9882	277.3	.99
1.7 I=-696.52 +35.11y -17605.4w +3.41P_{cm} (5.46)**(-3.25)* (1.42)	.9920	209.8	1.97
1.8 I=-3611.94 +23.71y +42.34P_{us} -1 (12.33)**(4.78)**	.9961	159.71	1.72
1.9 I=-2841.79 +29.86y +34.49P_{us} -1 -14.42dy (9.66)**(4.14)** (1.56) -5786.74w (1.45)	.9984	130.66	2.15

Where:
I = Annual dollar amount of U.S. direct investment in the EEC
y = Annual dollar GNP of the EEC
dy = Annual change in GNP of the EEC
P_{us} = Annual dollar amount of U.S. corporate profits before taxes
w = Wage differential ratio
k = U.S. company cost of capital estimate
T = Tariff distortion effect variable
P_{cm} = Annual profits from U.S. direct investments in the EEC, restated for petroleum profits.
The $\bar{R}^2$ is the coefficient of termination adjusted for degrees of freedom. The SE is the standard error of estimate of the regression equation. The DW is the Durbin-Watson measure of autocorrelation. The t-scores are indicated beneath their individual coefficients. The levels of significance are indicated by ** (.01 level) and * (.05 level).

110

explanatory variables, the significance ranking is as listed above,
with the two other tested variables having the correct theoretical
sign (positive for profitability of investment in Europe and negative
for the tariff distortion effect), but little statistical importance.
Equation 1.7 is the only equation in which another variable, profitability of U.S. investments, has any significance. Its t-score is
significant at the .2 level, but the t-score is probably overstated
because the equation is autocorrelated and is probably biased because
at least two more important variables were omitted.

The variable having a sign contrary to that of theoretical expectations is that of change in GNP, which was consistently negatively
correlated with I. A possible hypothesis for this relation would start
with the definition of book value. Book value is the excess of a firm's
assets in excess of its liabilities. It is increased by retained earnings
and new equity injections and decreased by losses and dividends.
Increases in profit levels of American companies in the EEC are
positively correlated with the change of GNP of the Six. In the time
period of this study, the simple correlation coefficient between these
two is .74. Since the business cycles of Western Europe and the
United States are often out of phase, it is possible, because of low
domestic cash generation, that the cash needs of the parent company
in the United States are greater in periods of rapid GNP growth
and high corporate profit levels of American subsidiaries in Europe.
The parent companies cause their European subsidiaries to remit
higher dividends than normal. This means in periods of high growth
and high U.S. direct investor profits in the EEC the book value of
these investments is negatively affected because of the high level of
dividends paid to the parent company in the U.S.

The author's opinion is that on theoretical and statistical
grounds the best equations for forecasting are probably 1.2, 1.8, and
1.9, which all have high $\bar{R}^2$, low standard errors of estimate and
little evidence of autocorrelation.

Appendix Table 2 presents the forecast book value of U.S. direct
investment in the EEC for 1969 and 1970 obtained by using the above-
mentioned three best predictive equations. The forecasts are compared with the actual book values for those years in order to rank
the predictive ability of the equations.[28] From the table the following
conclusions can be drawn:

1. The equations provide very accurate forecasts for 1969,
which is the nearest year to the 1958-68 time period from which
the equations were derived. All three equations are accurate within
two standard errors of estimate of the predicting equation, while
equations 1.2 and 1.8 are accurate within a small fraction of one
standard error of estimate.

Actual and Predicted Book Value of U.S. Direct Investment in the EEC, 1969-70

(1) Equation	(2) Year	(3) SE of Equation ($ millions)	(4) Predicted Book Value of U.S. Direct Investment in the EEC ($ millions)	(5) Actual Book Value of U.S. Direct Investment in EEC ($ millions)	(6) Difference (4 - 5)	(7) Difference Expressed in Number of SE of Equation (6 ÷ 3)
1.2 $I = -2344.71$ $+ 33.17y$ $- 29.76dy$ $+ 29.73 P_{us}$ $- 8933.40w$	1969	181.8	10,150	10,194	44	.24
	1970	181.8	11,003	11,695	692	3.81
1.8 $I = -3611.94$ $+23.71y$ $+42.34P_{us}-1$	1969	159.7	10,195	10,194	1	.01
	1970	159.7	11,220	11,695	475	2.97
1.9 $I = -2841.79$ $+29.86y$ $+34.49P_{us}-1$ $-14.42dy$ $-5786.74w$	1969	130.7	10,418	10,194	224	1.71
	1970	130.7	11,475	11,695	220	1.68

Where:
  I = Dollar value of U.S. direct investment in the EEC
  y = Annual dollar GNP of the EEC
  dy = Annual dollar change in GNP of the EEC
  P_{us} = Annual dollar amount of U.S. corporate profits before taxes
  w = Wage differential ratio.

2. The forecasts obtained in 1970 were more inaccurate for two of the three equations, with equations 1.2 and 1.8 having under-predicted the actual book value by almost four and three standard errors of estimate of the predicting equation, respectively. Equation 1.9 was the best forecasting equation having underpredicted the actual book value by less than two standard errors.

3. In general, the forecasting ability of the equations in 1969 and 1970 was identically correlated with their explanatory power over the 1958-68 period. Equation 1.9 had the highest $\bar{R}^2$ and the lowest SE over the 1958-68 period and similarly predicted both 1969 and 1970 book values within two standard errors of the 1958-68 estimate. Equation 1.8, which had the second highest $\bar{R}^2$ and second lowest SE in the 1958-68 period, was the best forecasting equation for 1969 book value and provided a 1970 estimate that was within three standard errors of the actual. Equation 1.2, which had the third highest $\bar{R}^2$ and the third lowest SE was the third ranked equation in predicting 1969 and 1970 actual book values. The 1969 estimate was highly accurate, but the 1970 forecast was only accurate to within four standard errors.

Variables Affecting the Changes in Book Values
of U.S. Direct Investment

Appendix Table 3 shows the results of a series of single equation models formulated using both stepwise and normal OLS methods to determine the importance of variables affecting the change in book value of U.S. direct investment in the EEC. The results are less satisfactory than those of the previous model, with lower $\bar{R}^2$, higher standard errors of estimate relative to the magnitude being estimated, and significant autocorrelation in the residuals.

The results reported by S & M were more satisfactory than those obtained by the author. For example, the regression for dI in terms of GNP as the only explanatory variable, yielded $\bar{R}^2$ of .959, which was significant at the .01 level with no autocorrelation for S & M.[29] The results obtained in this study showed an $\bar{R}^2$ of .432, which was significant at the .05 level with a DW score of 1.34.

There are two reasons why these results were so divergent. First, the time periods measured were different. S & M studied the 1952-66 period, while this study is concerned with 1958-68. This does not entirely explain the differences, because S & M also broke down their data into 1952-58 and 1959-66 periods. In the latter period, which closely corresponds to the time series of this study, S & M obtained $\bar{R}^2$ of .945, which was significant at the .01 level.[30] A second, more important, reason is that data used in each study was different. This study relied on the U.S. Department of Commerce

APPENDIX TABLE 3

Changes in Book Value of U.S. Investment in the EEC
and Various Explanatory Variables

Equation	$\bar{R}^2$	SE	DW
2.1 dI = -3340.91 -7.1223y +15336.09w +323.0k (-3.78)**(4.99)** (3.27)*	.8663	104.4	3.12
2.2 dI = -1983.51 -6.7437y +15898.53w (-2.41)* (3.48)**	.7096	155.5	2.94
2.3 dI = -3911.67 -13948.4w-7.55y +344.2k (3.98)** (1.81) (2.93)* +.604P_{cm} +1772.8T (.53) (.74)	.8519	117.2	2.70
2.4 dI = -3252.68 -9.5778y +15449.6w +328.58k (-2.01) (4.12)** (3.04)* +5.085dy +.760P_{cm} (.72) (.57)	.8673	112.4	2.73
2.5 dI = -1687.13 +10884w +6.68dy -1.59P_{cm} (2.67)* (.59) (1.74)	.6574	180.5	2.44
2.6 dI = -36.23 +2.757y (2.93)*	.4320	232.5	1.34
2.7 dI = -60.12 +1.784y +12.93dy (1.26) (.92)	.4227	234.4	1.22
2.8 dI = -20.738 +12.166P_{us} -1 (2.71)*	.3879	241.46	1.27
2.9 dI = -3783.68 +15414.07w +358.47k -1 (5.49)** (3.86)** -3.45y -1.61P_{cm} -1 (1.18) (1.55)	.8854	95.35	1.11

Where:
dI = Annual change in dollar amount of U.S. direct investment in the EEC
y = Annual dollar GNP of the EEC
dy = Annual change in GNP of the EEC
P_{us} = Annual dollar amount of U.S. corporate profits before taxes
w = Wage differential ratio
k = U.S. company cost of capital estimate
T = Tariff distortion effect variable
P_{cm} = Annual profits from U.S. direct investments in the EEC, restated for petro-leum profits.
   The $\bar{R}^2$ is the coefficient of determination adjusted for degrees of freedom. The SE is the standard error of estimate of the regression equation. The DW is the Durbin-Watson measure of autocorrelation. The t-scores are indicated beneath their individual coefficients. The levels of significance are indicated by ** (.01 level) and * (.05 level).

114

figures on book value of U.S. foreign direct investment as reported
annually in the Survey of Current Business.[31] Although the annual
changes in book value are similar for many years, there are several
years in the period that are very different.[32]

The best results obtained were $\bar{R}^2$ of .8663 for equation 2.1 and
.8854 and equation 2.9. In all the regressions for the 1958-68 period,
the explanatory variables for changes in book value that performed
the best were the wage differential variable (w) and the market size
variable (Y). The variable representing the cost of capital for U.S.
corporations (k) was also significant at the .01 level in equation 2.9
and at the .05 level in equation 2.1. The equations formulated after
the S & M hypothesis (equations 2.6 and 2.7) provided very low $\bar{R}^2$
of .4320 and .4227, respectively. In the 1958-68 period, the three
explanatory variables having the most statistical importance were
the wage differential, the market size, and the cost of capital variables.

In spite of the high $\bar{R}^2$ obtained from the two best models, the
author tends to view these formulations with suspicion. The important
explanatory variable of market size changes sign from equation to
equation. This may be seen from a comparison of equations 2.1 and
2.9 on one hand, and 2.6 and 2.7 on the other. Other explanatory
variables such as profits in the Common Market (P_{cm}) also have
sign changes, as may be observed by comparing equations 2.4 and
2.5. In addition, the sign of the variables in the best performing
equations are contrary to theoretical expectations. Equation 2.1
states that changes in book value are negatively correlated with
income levels in the EEC and positively correlated with wage differentials and the cost of capital variables. Equation 2.8 also has these
same puzzling signs and adds a fourth: that profits from U.S. investment in the EEC (lagged one year) are also negatively correlated
with changes in book value.

The two best equations for the 1958-68 period, equations 2.1
and 2.9, are highly inaccurate forecasting equations for 1969 and 1970
changes in book value. For example, the predicted increases in
book values of U.S. foreign investment in the EEC obtained by using
equation 2.1 are $353 million for 1969 and $478 million for 1970. The
actual increases in book values were $1,182 million in 1969 and
$1,501 million in 1970. Equation 2.9 was even more inaccurate, esti-
mating an increase in book value of $214 million in 1969 and a re-
duction of $20 million in 1970.

Equation 2.1 was also estimated using the standard GLS (gen-
eralized least squares) transformation procedure for reducing the
amount of autocorrelation.[33] The autocorrelation was reduced, but
the predictions generated by the transformed equations were not
improved over the OLS model.

Using equations 2.6 and 2.7, which were the functional forms recommended by S & M, improves the forecasting performance markedly. Equation 2.6, which relates changes in book value only to changes in Common Market GNP, provided estimates of $1,798 million in 1969 and $2,089 in 1970. Equation 2.7, which adds the explanatory variables of increase in Common Market GNP, improves the forecast to $1,351 million in 1969 and $1,545 million in 1970.

It is clear that the results of the models formulated to explain and predict changes in book value of U.S. direct investment in the Common Market have not been satisfactory. The best models gave high $\overline{R}^2$, but also evidenced autocorrelation and had important explanatory variables with signs contrary to theoretical expectations. In addition, these models derived from the 1958-68 period were inaccurate predictors of changes in book value in 1969 and 1970.

Conclusions

1. The best models formulated to predict book value of U.S. direct investment in the EEC provided very satisfactory results, with very high $\overline{R}^2$, little evidence of autocorrelation, and provided accurate predictions for 1969 and 1970 book values.

These models pointed up the importance of certain explanatory variables, omitted from previous research, such as levels of U.S. corporate profits (before income tax) and wage differentials. The most important explanatory variable in previous studies—market size—was confirmed in its importance in this study. Finally, other variables tested such as the dollar profit level of U.S. direct investments, tariff effects, and a proxy variable for an average American corporation's cost of capital were found to have little statistical significance.

2. Although the best models formulated are accurate predictors of book value of U.S. direct investment in the EEC, the author does not believe these models necessarily explain the causes of such investment. In particular, the author believes that the previous research has not placed sufficient attention on the role of expected profit, or expected cash generation as a determinant of new investments. In addition to the problem mentioned earlier of transfer pricing and profit allocation in the multinational corporation, the lack of data available on U.S. direct investment in the EEC does not allow the statistical formulation of a meaningful measure of expected profitability. The fact that return on equity was lower for U.S. investments in the EEC than for domestic U.S. investment for a short period does not necessarily mean that such investments are less profitable. Since investments are undertaken in order to create future cash flows, any

measurement concept that relates current investment to current
income, such as return on equity, is not an adequate explanation of
the reasons for marginal investment. In addition, the return on equity
concept omits consideration of the role of financial leverage in the
expected profitability of investments. For example, if a $100 invest-
ment financed by retained earnings yields a return of $10, then the
return on equity for this investment is 10 percent. If the same investment is financed $90 with new debt and only $10 with equity and the
return of the investment after interest charges is $4, then the return
on equity for this marginal investment is 40 percent.

  In conclusion, the author's opinion is that previous studies
have understated the role of expected profitability as a motive force
in the investment decision. Unfortunately, better statistical formulations must await the publication of more complete data.

  3. The best models formulated to predict the changes in book
value had high R^2 but also evidenced autocorrelation. In addition,
many explanatory variables exhibited signs contrary to theoretical
expectations. In the 1958-68 period, wage differentials and the cost
of capital variable (lagged one year) were the most significant statistical variables. The variable for market size—the most significant
factor in previous research—was of lesser importance in this study.
The predictive ability of the best models was very low in forecasting
1969 and 1970 changes in book value. The predictive power using
models that had performed well in previous research was considerably
higher, despite the low $\bar{R}^2$ obtained from these models in the 1958-68
period.

  4. The inconclusive nature of the results obtained for changes
in book value suggest that other approaches might be more fruitful.
An example of such an approach would be to disaggregate changes
in book value by actions that affect changes in book value and then
attempt to quantify these. Book value is increased by new equity
or by retained earnings and is reduced by dividends and losses.
The results obtained in this study suggest that the share of total
change in book value of these four components may have shifted over
time. For example, the U.S. government's controls on foreign direct
investment may have had the effect of limiting new equity additions
and retained earnings in EEC investments while encouraging an
increased level of dividend payments back to the U.S. There also
could have been concurrent policy changes on the part of several
EEC governments that had the effect of limiting non-American investments in the Community to a level below what it would have been without restriction.

  Another possibility is to examine whether changes in the tax
treatment of American subsidiaries by individual EEC countries, particularly with regard to withholding taxes on dividends, has affected

book value of direct investment. There are many such possibilities to be considered and more research on them is required before a more convincing empirical explanation of the determinants of change in book value of U.S. direct investment in the EEC can be formulated.

CHAPTER 1

1. See Robert A. Mundell, "International Trade and Factor Mobility" in his International Economics (New York: Macmillan, 1968), pp. 85-99 for a discussion of the effects of protection on factor mobility.

2. Calculated by the author from U.S. Department of Commerce, Survey of Current Business, October, 1971, pp. 32-33. The Survey figures for the September, 1957 issue were used as a base.

3. Calculated by author from International Monetary Fund (IMF), International Financial Statistics, April, 1972.

4. A recent estimate of the size of this "financial multiplier" puts the size of local capital at three to six times the incoming investment flow for France during the period 1954-64. See G. Y., Bertin, L'Investissement International (Paris: Presses Universitaires de France, 1967), p. 49.

5. Dr. Luc Wauters, President of the Executive Committee of Kredietbank, in a speech before the Belgian-American Chamber of Commerce at the St. Regis-Sheraton Hotel in New York City on September 29, 1967, places the figure at 17 percent for the period 1959-66. He also cites a survey by the Belgian National Bank that from 1958-65 the foreign companies provided 38 percent of their own capital, borrowed an additional 16 percent outside of Belgium, and the remaining 46 percent in Belgium.. The incoming amounts of foreign investment were BF (Belgian francs) 7.1 billion and 7.0 billion for 1965 and 1966 respectively (Belgian balance of payments statistics before 1965 did not break out direct investments separately, while those after 1968 would be exceptionally low owing to U.S. capital export restrictions and higher Eurobond interest rates.) If the national Bank's average locally borrowed figure is accepted, then the total foreign investment in Belgium in 1965 and 1966 would be BF 10.4 and 10.2 billion respectively. The total industrial capital formation for those two years was BF 48.3 billion for 1965 and BF 56.0 billion for 1966, indicating that the foreign percentage of total would be 21.6 percent for 1965 and 18.3 percent for 1966. These figures are substantiated by The Economist, which places American investment in Belgian manufacturing as 19 percent of that country's total in 1966. This is probable because the other component of industrial investment is in the extractive industries sector and this is almost entirely done by the Belgians. The American percentage

of total new investment was consistently over 70 percent in the
period 1959-67. For figures on Belgian capital formation, see
National Bank of Belgium, Bulletin d'Information et de Documenta-
tion, June, 1969, Table I-4a, Composition of the Belgian National
Product. For the incoming investment flows, see ibid., Table IX-1,
General Balance of Payments. For The Economist's figures, see
The Economist, March 23, 1968, p. 83. For the American percentage
of total new foreign investment in Belgium, see Ministry of Economic
Affairs, L'Investissement Etrangers en Belgique, 1968 report.

6. The food sector in general presents the most marked con-
trast between the United States and Europe. Except for the Anglo-
Dutch Unilever Company there is not a single European food
manufacturer that had sales of $400 million in 1965. In 1963 there
were twenty-four in the United States. See Christoper Layton,
L'Europe et les Investissements Americains Paris: Gallimard,
1968). (Originally published in English by the Atlantic Institute
under the title TransAtlantic Investments) [Paris: 1967], pp. 120-23.

Research conducted into the American penetration of the Belgian food sector estimated that American firms account for 60
percent of frozen fish sales and are expanding rapidly in all sectors
of the food industry. See Philippe Lousberg, "La Participation
Americain a l'Industrie Alimentaire Belge," L'Echo de la Bourse
(Brussels), November 30, 1967.

7. Before depreciation for 1968 the chemical sector had BF
80 billion of investment, 27 billion of which were foreign and almost
all of the foreign was American. See L'Economie Belge en 1968
(Brussels: Ministry of Economic Affairs), p. 124.

8. Lamfalussy defines defensive investment as an investment
policy that allocates increasingly scarce investment resources
to industries with falling demand and profit margins. Defensive
investment is opposed to enterprise investment that is carried out
in sectors with growing markets and high profit margins. Lamfalussy calculated normal profit rates for each sector and compared
this result with actual profit rates. Those industries that returned
substantially less than the normal profit rate were classified as
defensive investment industries, those at slightly below or equal
to normal profit were borderline industries, and those that returned
higher than normal profits were industries with enterprise investment. The normal profits were calculated by the addition of
equivalent quality corporate bond paper (the risk premium to the
outsider for holding the company's paper) with the entrepreneur's
risk premium, which is related to the variance of the individual
company rate of return for his sector with the mean rate of return
for the total Belgian industrial structure, Finally, the contribution
of each of the three types of investment to total Belgian industrial

investment was obtained by the summation of all investment made
defensive sectors, borderline sectors, and enterprise sectors.
Defensive sectors were coal mining, textiles, and basic metals.
The largest borderline sector was food, and the enterprise sectors
were electrical engineering, chemicals, and electricity and gas.
Lamfalussy's definitions are in his Investment and Growth in
Mature Economies: The Case of Belgium (New York: Macmillan,
1961), pp. xiv-xvi; his calculations for the rate of return by sector
are on p. 131; and his conclusions as to the weighting of the various
types of investments are on pp. 151-54.

9. For a description of the effects of increased domestic demand
on production in Belgium in the 1960-64 years, see "Belgium-
Luxumbourg Economic Survey" (pans: Organization for Economic
Cooperation and Development, 1964), pp. 8-13.

10. See Ira O. Scott, European Capital Markets (New York:
McGraw-Hill, 1968), p. 127.

11. See Pearson Hunt, Charles M. Williams, and Gordon
Donaldson, Basic Business Finance (Homewood, Ill.: Richard D.
Irwin, 1966. Sources of funds were calculated by the author from
balance sheets of all U.S. corporations in Basic Business Finance
(p. 12).

12. Calculated by author from International Monetary Fund,
International Financial Statistics, April, 1972, p. 60.

13. The effects of trade creation and diversion on Belgium by
the creation of the Common Market are far beyond the scope of
this study. Two of the best works on the subject are both by Don
D. Humphrey—see his The United States and the Common Market
(New York: Praeger, 1964) and for a brief description of the trade
creation and diversion process, see "Some Implications of Planning
for Trade and Capital Movements," paper presented at a Conference
of the Universities—National Bureau Committee for Economic
Research, National Bureau of Economic Research (New York:
Columbia University Press, 1967)

14. This figure and all those pertaining to Belgian exports are
from L'Economie Belge en 1970, (Brussels: Ministry of Economic
Affairs); pp. 362-63, with the totals calculated by the author.

15. Figures are calculated from data provided by the Ministry
of Economic Affairs, Institut National de Statistique, Annuaire
Statistique de la Belgique 1970, p 38. There is also a small
German-speaking population of 62,000 (.6 percent of total population)
that has been excluded from the above figures.

16. Calculated by the author from the data provided by the
Ministry of Economic Affairs by dividing the provincial GPP by
the figures for provincial population.

17. There is an unusual statistical distribution of per capita GDP at factor cost on both the high and low tails of the distribution. In a normal "student t" distribution of nine items, the t score for a 1 percent level of significance is 3.25. The t scores for the provinces on both the high and low per capita income figures exceeded this score, with Brussels at 5.90 and Limburg at 3.60. For a small sample of nine items the probability that two of them would be so dispersed is very small. The t test (also called the student t distribution) is a small sample version of the z score test. It is used for samples of under thirty items because smaller samples normally have larger tails, and hence the t scores for any given level of significance are higher than are the z scores. See Kong Chu, Principles of Econometrics, (Scranton: International Textbook, 1968), International Textbook Company, p. 13 or C. I. Chase, Elementary Statistical Procedures, 1967, pp. 133-36.

18. L. H. Klaassen, Area Economic and Social Redevelopment (Paris: Organization for Economic Cooperation and Development, 1965).

19. Klaassen, Ibid., p. 31.

20. This again refers to the student t test discussed previously. The significant values for a distribution of nine items is 4.78 at the .001 level and 3.25 at the 1 percent level. The actual t scores were 5.91 for Brabant and 3.60 for Limburg. See Chase, op. cit., p. 232, Table 111, Probability of t Distribution.

CHAPTER 2

1. See Ministry of Economic Affairs, Industrial Investment in Belgium—A Practical Guide (Brussels, 1968), p. 58.

2. Societe Generale de Banque, Industrial Investment in Belgium (Brussels, 1967), p. 73.

3. Industrial Investment in Belgium, op. cit.

4. Ibid.

5. Translated by the author from the original text of the law. Belgian Chamber of Representatives-218 (1965-66), No. 5, p. 41.

6. Ibid.

7. Industrial Investment in Belgium, op. cit., p. 59.

8. Societe Generale de Banque, "Government Aid for Investment in Belgium" (Brussels, 1968), p. 6.

9. Ibid., pp. 5-6.

10. Belgian Chamber of Representatives, op. cit., p. 5

11. There are many descriptions of the workings of the Belgian investment incentive program. Among the best the author has found are Ministry of Economic Affairs, Industrial Investment in Belgium—A Practical Guide and "Summary of Incentives to Foreign Investment in Belgium" (Brussels, 1968); Societe Generale de Banque,

"Government Aid for Investment in Belgium" (Brussels, 1968) and
its Industrial Investment in Belgium (Brussels, 1967); Kredietbank
Belgium—Key to the Common Market (Brussels, 1966); Banque de
Bruxelles, Belgium—Land of Investments (Brussels, 1965); Arthur
Anderson & Company, A Tax and Trade Guide to Belgium (New
York, 1967).

   12. The investors qualifying for an interest rate subsidy may
borrow from either private or semipublic bodies. The only constraint is that if a private institution is selected, the total of interest
and finance charges cannot exceed the amount that the semiprivate
body would have charged for an equivalent time and risk. The
largest semiprivate financial institution in Belgium is the SNCI
(Societe Nationale de Credit à l'Industrie), which was founded in
1919 and is funded by the sale of bonds that are guaranteed by
the state. It is autonomous in its management and does not take
equity positions in investments. It had credit outstanding of $1.38
billion in 1966. For an explanation of the SNCI and other semi-
official Belgian financial institutions, see Financing Business in
Belgium (New York: Morgan Guarantee Bank and Trust Company,
1965).

   13. Figures are from Industrial Investment in Belgium, op. cit.,
p. 59-60.

   14. The persistent rise in Belgian interest rates illustrates
the problem of a small country with a highly open economy and
convertible currency maintaining an independent monetary policy.
In March, 1969, the rates on the Eurodollar market were two
percentage points over domestic Belgian interest rates. The
result was that there was strong downward pressure of the Belgian
franc because of people borrowing francs at low rates, converting
them into dollars, and then lending them on the Eurodollar market
and gaining a significant spread. The effect of this has been con-
tinuous upward movement of Belgian interest rates throughout
1969. For press reports of this, see Clyde H. Farnsworth,
"Europeans Facing a Dollar Shortage," New York Times, March 5,
1969, p. 51. The SNCI rates are from L'Echo de la Bourse (Brussels), October 19, 1969.

   15. Calculated from explanations of the workings of the laws,
Industrial Investment in Belgium, op. cit., pp. 59-60.

   16. Ibid., page 60.

   17. This information concerning the practical workings of the
direct grant and interest rate subsidies was given to me by Charles
Van Overstraeten at the Belgian Consulate in New York City.

   18. Some of the reasons are the following: For American firms,
which made up 70 percent of the new foreign investment since 1959,
the restriction on capital exports from the United States had meant

heavier reliance on local capital markets. For all foreign firms, Belgian interest rates have been 2-3 percent under Eurobond rates for equivalent periods. In addition, for reasons of corporate finance, many firms prefer to have most liabilities denominated in the same currency as income, which for a Belgian foreign subsidiary is Belgian francs. This avoids the loss to company net worth that results when a devaluation occurs to a foreign subsidiary whose income stream is in local currency and whose liabilities are in dollars. Finally, if a company can put in a small capital base and leverage itself highly with the aid of the State Guarantee, the resulting income stream would be larger than could be normally earned with a small capital base and a normal debt-equity ratio. With this small capital base and relatively large income stream the return on investment is very high with the resulting benefits to the company's earnings per share. Finally, the Foreign Direct Investment program administered by the Department of Commerce places limitations on the amount of capital that can be exported from the United States. Because of this program, foreign borrowings have been the primary means of financing the U.S. direct investment in Europe since 1968. Since foreign expansion must be financed by foreign borrowing for American firms, foreign borrowing at subsidized rates becomes extremely attractive. The information on the financing of U.S. operations in Europe is from D. I. Katz, Director of the Office of Foreign Direct Investment, Department of Commerce, at the seminar "Foreign Direct Investment Programs" sponsored by the Conference Board at the Waldorf-Astoria Hotel, New York City, February 17, 1971. For the corporate finance aspects see D. B. Zenaff J. Zwick, International Financing Management (Englewood Cliffs, N.J.: Prentice-Hall, 1969), pp. 228-49.

19. Interest expense is tax deductible in Belgium up to the 9 percent rate. See Arthur Anderson & Company, A Tax and Trade Guide to Belgium, op. cit., page 53.

20. "Uncovered" refers to that part of the loan left over after the lender has received security, in the form of mortgages or guarantees, from the borrower that is less than the total amount of the loan. See SNCI, "Credit à l'Industrie" (Brussels, 1968) for a description of the workings of the program.

21. In addition to the tax advantages mentioned in connection with the 1959 and 1966 laws, the government created special tax advantages by the Royal Decree of April 18, 1967 that limited the taxation of corporate dividends, ended the time limitation on the carryforward of losses, and provided for exemption from taxes for certain acquisitions and mergers. This decree has limited relevance to the regional development program and is presented here only to maintain the completeness of the study. For details

of the State Guarantee and the tax exemptions, see Industrial
Investment in Belgium, op. cit., pp. 60-61.

    22. See Arthur Anderson & Company, op. cit., pp. 48 and 50-51.

    23. Industrial Investment in Belgium, op. cit., p. 61.

    24. This is the viewpoint expressed to the author during meetings
with Belgian officials in Brussels and New York in March, 1968 and
December, 1969, respectively. In addition it is stated in Ministry
of Economic Affairs, "Summary of Incentives to Foreign Investment
in Belgium," op. cit., p. 4.

    25. Adapted with present interest rates and the addition of Case
III from "Summary of Incentives to Foreign Investment," op. cit.,
p. 8.

    26. See Business International, January 19, 1968, p. 17.

CHAPTER 3

    1. See Jacques Hollander, Les Investissements Americains en
Belgique Brussels: Les Editions du Centre Paul Hymans, 1963),
pp. 12-53.

    2. For theoretical proof of this argument, see Robert A.
Mundell, "International Trade and Factor Mobility," in his International Economics (New York: Macmillan, 1968), pp. 85-99.
Another argument is that the market size of the EEC that offered
significant economies of scale to the giant American investors was
the vital factor. Scaperlanda and Mauer, using regression analysis,
have concluded that market size of the EEC was the vital factor.
See Scaperlanda, Anthony E. and Mauer Laurence J., "Determinants
of U.S. Direct Investment in the EEC," American Economic Review,
September, 1969, pp. 558-68. For the author's study, see the
appendix to this book.

    3. See particularly Articles 12-17 of the Treaty of Rome.

    4. See the Treaty of Rome, Articles 17-19.

    5. This assumes the hypothetical investor is not concerned
with the long-term benefits. This is a reasonable assumption
because with the use of the present value method to analyze investment decisions, $1 of profit in the tenth year of operations is worth
only $.39 today using a 10 percent after-tax discount base. This
is an average discount factor for investments in stable developed
countries. See Robert B. Stobaugh, Jr., "How to Analyze Foreign
Investment Climates," Harvard Business Review, September-
October, 1969, p. 101. The use of discounted cash flow methods,
increasingly prevalent in larger companies, makes long-run
investment decisions more difficult to justify because the longer
the term until high profits are achieved, the smaller the present
value of that profit.

6. Calculated from the U.S. Department of Commerce's annual
Survey of Current Business, which deals with the U.S. investment
position abroad. The individual articles are not cited because they
are so numerous, but it is normally the October issue, although
certain annual articles, as in 1958, appeared in September.

7. See Belgian Ministry of Economic Affairs, L'Investissement
Etrangers en Belgique (Brussels, 1968, 1969, 1970 report), pp. ix-x,
to see that the Belgian government is of this opinion.

8. Calculated by author from Institut National de Statistique,
Bulletin de Statistique, April, 1969, p. 114.

9. These figures were calculated from L'Investissement
Etrangers en Belgique, report 1969, 1970, op. cit., p. xii. The
table from which they were taken breaks down investment into new
foreign investment, new Belgian investment, and existing investment
benefiting from subsidies. There are two problems in comparing
this information directly with the information in figure 3 to arrive
at a conclusion concerning the amount of foreign investment that
benefits from subsidies in any one year. First, the existing investment category may already include large number of foreign firms.
Second, the time period referred to in the two sets of figures is
different. The figure for new foreign investment is the amount of
investment the foreign firms will make in a year. The amount of
investment that qualifies for incentives is dated by the decision of
the government to give them incentives. Hence, a new foreign
investment made in December, 1967, for which the decision to
grant incentives was made in January, 1968, would be a 1967 new
investment but a 1968 investment benefiting from incentives.
Because these statistics are published by two different departments
(the first by the Department of the Direction of Foreign Investment
and the second by the Department of Economic Expansion and
Development), the figures probably never will be reconciled.

10. Ibid., Table 6, Rapport 1968, 1969, 1970

11. Ibid., Table 6, Rapport 1968, 1969, 1970

12. Ibid., Table 6, Rapport, 1968, 1969, 1970

13. See L'Investissements Etrangers en Belgique, 1970 report,
op. cit., Table 2, p. viii.

14. New foreign industrial investment in this period was BF
57.3 billion out of a total of 65.5 billion. See ibid.

15. The plant locations were made by the author from the lists
of new plant locations provided in L'Investissement Etrangers en
Belgique, op. cit., which are grouped by nationality.

16. By law no Belgian corporation can be a 100 percent foreign
subsidiary. There must be nominal Belgian holdings of stock.
See Arthur Anderson & Company, A Tax and Trade Guide to Belgium
(New York, 1967), page 12.

17. By author's calculation from the lists of plant locations mentioned in note 15.

18. Calculated from plant locations in L'Investissement Etranger en Belgique by the author.

19. Despite the fact that only 106 of the 273 new plant locations between 1967 and 1970 were American, Americans invested BF 25.0 billion of the total BF 57.2 billion in industrial investments (44 percent). Calculated by the author from L'Investissement Etrangers en Belgique, 1968 and 1970 reports, Table 2, page xiii.

20. This figure and those following it concerning the location of new plants by size of investment were calculated by the author from the lists of the locations of new foreign investment in L'Investissements Etrangers en Belgique, 1967 and 1970 reports.

21. The correlation coefficient computed was the Spearman rho correlation for ranked data, which is

$$r = 1 - \frac{6x \; d^2}{n(n^2-1)}$$

where r = coefficient of correlation

d^2 = the difference between the rankings squared

n = the number of observations (seven for this problem)

See B. Parl, Basic Statistics (New York: Doubleday, 1967), pp. 261-67 for a discussion of rank order correlations.

22. J.F. Due, and R.W. Clower, Intermediate Economic Analysis (Homewood, Ill. Richard D. Irwin, 1961), p. 149.

23. For a discussion of the importance of this factor to the United States, see Don D. Humphrey, The United States and the Common Market (New York: Praeger 1964), pp. 123-28.

24. See Humphrey, op. cit., pp. 126-28.

25. See for example, the article in L'Echo de la Bourse (Brussels), November 30, 1967, by Philippe Lousberg on "La participation Americain à l'Industrie Alimentaire Belge."

26. For an example of this, see the famous business school case. "The Case of the Unidentified Industries," in which the fixed asset/total asset ratio varies between 6.8 percent and 89.9 percent, depending on the industry. This case is described in Pearson Hunt, Charles Williams, Gordon and Donaldson, Basic Business Finance (Homewood, Ill. Richard D. Irwin, 1966), pp. 664-66.

27. See C.I. Chase, Elementary Statistical Procedures p. 235.

28. See Robert B. Stobaugh, Jr., "Where in the World Should We Put That Plant," Harvard Business Review, January-February, 1969, pp. 129-36. Stobaugh finds that the four country-related variables to determining foreign investment are market size, investment climate, availability of local technology or know-how, and distance from the major producing countries. Countries that have the worst combination of these four variables will tend to

have a much greater product imitation lag than those with an
optimum combination.

29. American subsidiaries resident in Belgium, can, for example,
invest in the other member countries of the EEC and benefit from
rights of establishment that are guaranteed to intracommunity
investment by Article 58 of the Treaty of Rome. See W. H.
Balekjian, Legal Aspects of Foreign Investment in the EEC
(Manchester: 1967), pp. 228-33.

30. The increasingly negative German opinion concerning
American investment reflected both management-labor disputes
(Deere-Lanz Tractors) and fears of excessive American control
in a vital industry (Socony-Mobil and GBAG, the coal mines). See
Christopher Layton, L'Europe et les Investissements Americains
(Paris: Gallimard, 1968), 59-86.

In France the issues were the same—labor disputes following
an American "rationalization" of production (General Motors and
Remington-Rand) and fear of American control of a vital industry
(Chrysler-Simca and General Electric and Machines Bull) and the
government reaction was stronger. See Allan W. Johnstone, United
States Direct Investment in France (Cambridge, Mass.: MIT Press),
1965.

In Italy, which has an antique industrial structure and a worse
problem of regional development than does Belgium, the government
has been favorable to foreign investment. Despite this there have
been a number of companies whose operations have failed in the
south of Italy. The latest and largest of these was the Raytheon
Corporation, which wrote off the $20 million investment in Italy
in 1968. See the New York Times, August 26, 1968, p. 55.

31. See Hollander, op. cit., map facing p. 160.

32. Calculated from map, ibid. It has already been shown that
there is no statistical difference between American and other foreign
investment in the 1967-68 sample. This analysis assumes this
condition also prevailed in 1957-61 and therefore a comparison
between these two periods can be made.

33. The 1957-61 figures are calculated by the author from the
map cited in Hollander, op. cit. The 1967-68 figures are calculated
by the author from his own investment locations by industry.

34. The figures were calculated from the map presented in
Hollander, op. cit. The 1967-70 figures were calculated by the
author and presented in Table 10 of this chapter.

35. The most efficient combination of a given value of factor
inputs yielding the largest possible output, which is the efficient
production function, is limited at any given time by the existing
technology. See J. M. Henderson and R. E. Quandt, Microeconomic
Theory (New York: McGraw-Hill, 1958), pp. 43-44.

36. This is true because of a common money and efficient capital market that keeps yields constant in any given country because of equilibrating capital flows. See T. Scitovsky, Economic Theory and Western European Integration (Stanford, Calif.: Stanford University Press, 1958), pp. 85-91.

37. See Balekjian, op. cit., pp. 248-49.

38. Ibid., p. 248.

39. For a more detailed discussion of the possible effects of tariff policy on regional development, see H. O. Nourse, Regional Economics (New York: McGraw-Hill, 1968), p. 230.

40. This definition of the real weight of a tariff policy upon a given domestic industry is derived from the concept of the real tariff. This in turn was taken from Humphrey, op. cit., pp. 60-63.

41. The labor force figures and the GPP were calculated by the author from Ministry of Economic Affairs, Industrial Investment in Belgium—A Practical Guide (Brussels, 1968), and the unemployment (which when divided by the labor force gives the unemployment rate) is from Bulletin de Statistique, op. cit., April-May, 1969, p. 466.

The synthetic welfare index for 1966 (the latest available) is calculated by the Economic Research Center of the University of Louvain using fifteen selected welfare indicators. These are: housing space, connection to sewage mains, baths and shower baths, central heating, degree of attendance at secondary schools, degree of attendance at vocational training institutions, male university students, female university students, medical equipment, new cars, telephones, telephones in worker's families, portable radios, TV sets, and personal care. The figures given are for the districts. The author added all the provincial totals by district and then averaged them to get the average provincial welfare index. See the Kredietbank Weekly Bulletin, March 16, 1968, article on "Regional Welfare Discrepancies in Belgium," pp. 97-101.

42. The fact that the marginal revenue product is lower in the high-labor industries in Belgium is shown by the fact that among the four industrial industries for which there is data given the most labor intensive industry (textiles) has the lowest average wage rate (BF 46.6 per hour in October, 1968,) while one of the least labor intensive (chemicals) has the highest wage rate (BF 61.5 per hour in October, 1968). See Bulletin de Statistique, April-May, 1969, p. 462.

43. For the best discussion of the various approaches utilized by economists with regard to regional analysis, see J. R. Meyer, "Regional Economics: A Survey," American Economic Review, Vol. 53 (1963), pp. 19-54.

44. "Input-Output Study of Liege," Revue Economique Wallon, September-October, 1969, pp. 61-69.

45. The traditional method of attempting to derive a regional multiplier is to utilize employment figures by region, assumes that these are proportionate to production, and then gets the national average employment in each industry. If the provincial employment on a proportional basis is less than the national, then it is assumed that this industry's products are imported into the region. The summation of this for all industries in all regions gives rise to a multiplier based on those provinces that have more exporting industries (basic employment industries) than importing industries (nonbasic employment industries). This technique is discussed in H.O. Nourse, op. cit., pp. 163-80 and Walter Isard, Methods of Regional Analysis (Cambridge, Mass.: MIT Press, 1960), pp. 189-205. The direct multiplier effect obtained from the basic employment industries is multiplied by the indirect effect of an increased unit of output (this is the same figure as the indirect multiplier effect for the industry in question obtained from national input-output tables) to get the total multiplier.

There are several grave limitations to this approach. First, by assuming employment is proportional to production one ignores the effects of productivity on interregional trade. Second, by deriving a multiplier from employment instead of incremental income, the multiplier definition is so changed as to make it meaningless. See C. L. Levin, "Regional and Inter-Regional Accounts in Perspective" Papers and Proceedings of the Regional Science Association, Vol. 13 (1964), pp. 127-44.

46. This is the traditional presentation of the regional multiplier as first discussed by L. A. Metzler, "A Multiple Region Theory of Income and Trade," Econometrica, October, 1950, pp. 329-54. The only change is that investment is defined to include only private investment and omitting government transfer payments, because the focus here is on the multiplier effects of the new foreign investment.

47. These are feasible size multipliers for the differences between less developed and more developed regions. See R. Vining, "The Region as an Economic Entity and Certain Variations to be Observed in the Study of Systems of Regions," Papers and Proceedings of the American Economic Association, Vol. 39 (May, 1969), and Isard, op. cit., pp. 205-13.

48. It should also be remembered that future multipliers depend on future investment. Kindleberger believes that the rate of future re-investment depends directly on the profitability of the investment in question. See Charles P. Kindleberger, American Business Abroad: Six Lectures on Direct Investment (New Haven: Yale University Press, 1969), p. 7.

49. Isard believes that for the textile industry it is the dominant locational consideration. See Isard, op. cit., p. 243.

50. The central geographic position of Belgium becomes even more important when it is recalled how much Belgian firms do export and how much of those exports go to the other Common Market countries. Belgian exports as a percentage of its GNP were 36 percent in 1967, with its EEC partners taking 64.3 percent of the total. On the average, foreign firms tend to export even more than do local ones, so that the central position of Belgium for these companies would be even more important. For the figures on the Belgian international trading position, see Chapter 1, pp. 9-10. For proof of the higher foreign propensity to invest, see Hollander, op. cit., p. 197.

51. For example, the per-unit railway traffic costs (in English pence) in 1961 were .364 for Belgium, .667 for Switzerland, .619 for West Germany, .449 for Holland, .443 for Italy, .538 for France, and .632 for Britain. See S. Joy, "Railway Track Costs," in Denys Munby, ed., Transport (Middlesex: Penguin Modern Economics Series, 1968), p. 146.

52. See Industrial Investment in Belgium: A Practical Guide, op. cit., p. 59.

53. This was the case for most of Europe in the two decades following World War II. See M. M. Postan, An Economic History of Western Europe 1945-64 (London: Macmillan, 1967), pp. 143-70.

54. Alexandre Lamfalussy, Investment and Growth in Mature Economies: The Case of Belgium (New York: Macmillan, 1961), pp. xiv-xv.

55. See Harry G. Johnson, Economic Policies Toward Less Developed Countries (New York: Praeger, 1967), pp. 84-104, 163-211.

CHAPTER 4

1. See, for example, Center for Studies in Vocational and Technical Education, University of Wisconsin, Madison and the Industrial Relations Centre, Queen's University, Kingston, Ontario, Cost-Benefit Analysis of Manpower Policies, Proceedings of a North American Conference, 1969; and Shlomo Reutlinger, Techniques for Project Appraisal under Uncertainty, World Bank Staff Occasional Paper No. 10, (Baltimore: Johns Hopkins University Press), 1970.

2. C. W. Hale, "The Optimality of Local Subsidies in Regional Development Programs," Quarterly Review of Business and Economics, Autumn, 1969, pp. 35-50.

3. See W. J. Baumol, "On the Social Rate of Discount," American Economic Review, September, 1968, pp 788-802.

4. Ibid., p. 791.
5. Ibid., pp. 798-99.

CHAPTER 5
1. See J. F. Due and R. W. Clower, Intermediate Economic Analysis (Homewood, Ill.: Richard D. Irwin, 1961), pp. 149-51.
2. The nature of transport costs of extra costs that limit low wage factors in the calculation of plant location is discussed extensively in Walter Isard, Methods of Regional Analysis, (Cambridge, Mass.: MIT Press, 1960), pp. 512-34.
3. Transportation industries are material oriented because of the limitations of technology in which large amounts of one material are consumed in the production of another, the classical example being coal and steel. The bulk of the product being consumed would have involved prohibitive transport costs for plant locations a great distance from the source of that product. Other types of industries, such as food, are weight-gaining industries, the transport costs for which would be prohibitive if the plant location were far from the sales market. This distinction of industries in which the transport costs play an important role is made in J. Freedman and W. Alonso, eds., Regional Development and Planning: A Reader (Cambridge, Mass.: MIT Press, 1964), pp. 98-100.
4. This possibility is mentioned by Alonso, ibid., but he does not consider it a likely situation in a developed country.
5. For example, E. F. Denison believes that only 5 percent of the total increase in growth in the 1950-62 period for nine major countries of Northwest Europe is because of educational improvements in the labor force during that period. See E. F. Denison, Why Growth Rates Differ (Washington, D.C.: Brookings Institution, 1967), Table 21-4, p. 301.
6. This is clear from Alonso's article "Location Theory," in Freedman and Alonso, op. cit., pp. 78-106.
7. The harmful effect of the minimum wage on employment in depressed areas in the United States is discussed by James M. Buchanan and John E. Moses in their "A Regional Countermeasure to National Wage Standardization," American Economic Review, June, 1960, pp. 434-38.
8. For example, even in developing countries one of the major impediments to satisfactory levels of employment is the insistence by foreign investors on using their same capital intensive technology that they use elsewhere in the developed world. The author does not wish to debate this conclusion, only to point out the trend toward fairly uniform capital labor ratios in the same industry in different countries. For a discussion of these trends, see Richard N. Cooper,

The Economics of Interdependence: Economic Policy in the Atlantic Community (New York: McGraw-Hill Paperbacks, 1968), pp. 68-76.

9. According to Don Humphrey, this is one "commonly overlooked advantage" of foreign investment to the host country because the tax revenue from the investment normally accrues to the host country with a corresponding loss of tax revenue by the country of the investing firm. See Don D. Humphrey, "Some Implications of Planning for Trade and Capital Movements," Paper presented at A Conference of Universities—National Bureau Committee for Economic Research, National Bureau of Economic Research (New York: Columbia University Press, 1967), p. 173.

10. See S. R. Ross and J. H. Guttentag, "United States Taxation of International Business Transactions," in W. S. Surrey and C. Shaw, eds., A Lawyer's Guide to International Business Transactions (Philadelphia: Joint Committee on Continuing Legal Education of the American Law Institute and the American Bar Association, 1963), pp. 719-840. See particularly pages 736-41 for a description of the derivative tax credit.

11. The $10 U.S. tax is calculated in the following manner: The U.S. tax on the entire amount of profit is $50. There is the $40 derivative tax credit, leaving a balance of $10 that must be paid to the U.S. government. This is the method utilized for the calculation of the tax burden in the developed countries in which U.S. firms have subsidiaries. See Ross and Guttentag, op. cit., p. 737.

12. This is the opinion of Professor W. S. Surrey of the Fletcher School, expressed in course Law 5b: International Legal Problems of Multi-National Trade and Investment, Fall Term, 1966.

13. See Cooper, op. cit., Table 6-1, p. 166.

14. Ibid.

15. Ibid.

16. The term extra depreciation is used here as the difference between the amount of depreciation obtained by the use of accelerated methods minus the amount obtained by the use of straight-line methods. For a description of the various depreciation methods and their calculation, see E. A. Spiller, Financial Accounting (Homewood, Ill.: Richard D. Irwin, 1966), pp. 252-67.

17. For a clear derivation of the tax savings from depreciation, see H. Bierman, Jr. and S. Smidt, The Capital Budgeting Decision (New York: Macmillan, 1971).

18. The reasoning concerning the impossibility of using depreciation as an efficient type of investment incentive is from William T. Hogan, Depreciation Reform and Capital Replacement (Washington, D.C.: American Enterprise Institute, September, 1962), pp. 47-52.

19. Sweden is the only country to use depreciation and tax benefits as major incentives to encourage foreign and domestic investment

in its depressed areas. The results were negative. See Martin
Schnitzer, The Swedish Investment Reserve: A Device for
Stabilization? (Washington, D.C.: American Enterprise Institute,
July, 1967), pp. 38-39.

20. Charles P. Kindleberger, American Business Abroad: Six
Lectures in Direct Investment (New Haven: Yale University Press,
1969), pp. 14-19.

21. See the Conference Board, Obstacles and Incentives to
Private Foreign Investment, 1967-68, Vol. II, Studies in Business
Policy, No. 130 (New York, 1969), p. 3.

22. Modified from Ministry of Economic Affairs "Summary of
Incentives to Foreign Investment" (Brussels, 1968), p. 4.

23. See for example, J. T. S. Potterfield, Investment Decisions
and Capital Costs (Englewood Cliffs, N.J.: Prentice-Hall, 1965),
pp. 20-41.

24. For a discussion of debt capacity relative to total services
of funds, see Pearson Hunt, Charles M. Williams, Gordon and
Donaldson, Basic Business Finance (Homewood, Ill.: Richard D.
Irwin, 1966), pp. 387-408.

25. This was one of the conclusions reached at the seminar
"Foreign Direct Investment Programs," sponsored by the Conference Board, Waldorf-Astoria Hotel, New York City, February
17, 1971.

26. These conversations took place with Belgian officials in
March, 1968 in Brussels and November, 1969 in New York.

27. The Canadian plan ties together the jobs created and the
subsidy on capital costs in a unique way. The basic limitation of
the subsidy is 20 percent of the capital costs (fixed assets plus
some working capital) plus $5,000 per worker employed. The
maximum of primary and secondary development incentives must
not be greater than $30,000 per each worker directly employed
in the new investment or $12 million. This encouraged the hiring
of workers until the maximum amount of the $12 million has been
met. See "Regional Development Incentives Act and the Regional
Development Incentives Regulations," Canadian House of Parliament,
Bill passed July 9, 1969, (Ottawa: Queen's Printer for Canada,
1969), pp. 4-8.

28. See Jean Marchand's speech, "Incentives for Regional
Economic Expansion," Remarks relating to the introduction of the
Regional Development Incentives Bill to the Canadian House of
Parliament, May 27, 1969, p. 3.

29. "Regional Development Incentives Act," op. cit., sections
10.1 and 10.2, p. 8.

30. Ibid.

31. For a description of the World Bank's recommendations in Singapore, see The Economist Intellegence Unit, No. 2 (1970), Singapore-Malasayia, pp. 11-12.

32. Calculated by author from Jacques Hollander, Les Investissements Americains en Belgique (Brussels: Editions du Centre Paul Hymans, 1963), map facing p. 160.

33. See Ronald B. Gold, "Subsidies to Industry in Pennsylvania," National Tax Journal, 19, no. 3 (September, 1966), 286-97.

34. Ibid., p. 290.

35. See Sar Levitan, Experiment on Trial (Baltimore: Johns Hopkins University Press, 1967).

36. The two studies that discuss the tax aspects of local incentives and their relative strength in relation to other cost considerations are John F. Due, "Studies of State-Local Tax Influence on the Location of Industry," National Tax Journal, 14, no. 2 (June, 1961), 167-73 and B. Bridges, Jr., "State and Local Inducements for Industry," National Tax Journal, 21, no. 2 (June, 1968), 183. The study that discusses regional incentives from the economic welfare aspect is Carl W. Hale, "The Optimality of Local Subsidies in Regional Development Programs," Quarterly Review of Business and Economics, Autumn, 1969, pp. 35-50.

37. For a good, short discussion of the reasons for depressed areas, see Cooper, op. cit., pp. 188-93. For a deeper treatment, see J. G. Williamson, "Regional Inequality and National Development: A Description of the Patterns," in W. L. Needleman, ed., Regional Analysis (Middlesex: Penguin Modern Economics Series, 1968), pp. 99-158.

38. See speech by Jean Marchand, Minister for Regional Economic Expansion, op. cit., p. 1.

39. See National Industrial Conference Board, op. cit., pp. 70-71.

40. See W. H. Balekjian, Legal Aspects of Foreign Investment in the EEC (Manchester: 1967), pp. 140-41. See also H. B. Chenery, "Development Policies for Southern Italy," Quarterly Journal of Economics, Vol. 76 (1962), pp. 515-47.

41. For a statistical examination of the strength of these factors on U.S. direct investment in Western Europe, see Scaperlanda, Anthony E. and Mauer, Laurence J., "Determinants of U.S. Direct Investment in the EEC," American Economic Review, September, 1969, pp. 558-68.

42. For Belgium, see Ministry of Economic Affairs, Industrial Investment in Belgium—A Practical Guide (Brussels, 1968), pp. 58-63. For Canada, the United Kingdom, and Italy, see the references listed in notes 38, 39, and 40.

43. The Quebec and Ontario programs were described in full-page advertisements in the Wall Street Journal, December 1, 1969.

These programs rely on the federal basic incentive, plus a small amount of provincial incentive as an extra inducement to select that province.

44. National Industrial Conference Board, op. cit., pp. 8-9.
45. See National Industrial Conference Board, op. cit., p. 26.

CHAPTER 6

1. See, for example, David B. Hertz "Risk Analysis in Capital Investment," Harvard Business Review, January-February, 1964; Shlomo Reutlinger, Techniques for Project Appraisal under Uncertainty, World Bank Staff Occasional Paper, No. 10 (Baltimore: Johns Hopkins University Press, 1970); and Hans. A. Adler, Economic Appraisal of Transport Projects (Bloomington: Indiana University Press, 1971).

2. For a discussion of present value and capital budgeting techniques widely used in various corporations, see Robert B. Stobaugh, "How to Analyze Foreign Investment Climates," Harvard Business Review, September-October 1969.

3. For a clear discussion of capital budgeting and the cost of capital see Bierman and Smidt, op. cit., chapters 8 and 9.

4. See Bierman and Smidt, op. cit., pp. 281-366.

APPENDIX

1. V. N. Bandera and J. T. White, "U.S. Direct Investments and Domestic Markets in Europe," Economia Internationale, August, 1968.

2. A. E. Scaperlanda and L. J. Mayer, "Determinants of U.S. Direct Investment in the EEC," American Economic Review, September, 1969.

3. The book value figure is from U.S. Department of Commerce, Survey of Current Business, "U.S. Direct Investments Abroad", Annual Article, 1956-71, Washington, D.C. (For a description of the transfer pricing mechanism in the petroleum industry, see note 15. pp. 180-84.)

4. C. P. Kindleberger, American Business Abroad, (New Haven and London: Yale University Press, 1969), pp. 60-62.

5. Draper and Smith, Applied Regression Analysis, (New York, London, and Sydney: John Wiley and Sons, 1966), pp. 163-95.

6. Survey of Current Business, op. cit.
7. Ibid.
8. International Monetary Fund, International Financial Statistics.
9. Ibid.
10. Survey of Current Business, op. cit.

11. Ibid., and United Nations, United Nations Statistical Yearbooks.

12. International Monetary Fund, Directions of Trade.

13. Ibid.

14. Survey of Current Business, op. cit. and Fortune Magazine, issues containing articles on 500 largest U.S. corporations, 1958-71.

15. Standard and Poor, Standard and Poor's Trade and Securities Index, 1971 (New York: S&P Publisher).

16. Kindleberger, op. cit., pp. 19-25, and A. E. Scaperlanda and L. J. Mayer, op. cit., pp. 560-61.

17. The average annual hourly wage in industry was obtained from UN Statistical Yearbooks. The Common Market figure was an average of its six member countries, weighted by the share of each in the book value of U.S. direct investments in the EEC. The EEC average was then divided by the U.S. average annual hourly wage in industry (also from UN Statistical Yearbooks) to arrive at the final ratio.

18. D. W. Jorgensen and C. D. Siebert, "A Comparison of Alternative Theories of Corporate Investment Behavior," American Economic Review, September, 1968.

19. R. A. Mundell, "International Trade and Factor Mobility", American Economic Review, June, 1957.

20. A. E. Scaperlanda and L. J. Mayer, op. cit.

21. Don D. Humphrey, "Some Implications of Planning for Trade and Capital Movements", A Conference of the Universities-National Bureau Committee for Economic Research, National Bureau of Economic Research (New York and London: Columbia University Press, 1967).

22. The book value figure for petroleum investment in the EEC was obtained from Survey of Current Business, op. cit. It was assumed that this book value earned the average return on equity received by the petroleum industry that year, as taken from Fortune Magazine, op. cit. In order to avoid double counting, the restated return on investment was netted against the petroleum industry's actual return. This residual figure was added to the U.S. investors' return, excluding petroleum, to arrive at a total industry return.

23. C. Tugendhat, Oil: The Biggest Business (London: Egre and Spottiswoode, 1968), pp. 180-84.

24. Standard and Poor, op. cit.

25. Ibid.

26. While there is considerable discussion as to the best theoretical formulation of the cost of equity capital, the traditional formulation proposed by most authors is

$$k = \frac{Do}{Po} + g$$

where k = the after-tax cost of equity capital
      Do = dividends per share in the current year
      Po = the current market price per share in the current year
       g = the expected annual percentage growth rate in dividends
           for future years.

For a more detailed discussion, see any good text, such as pp. 20-51.

27. Ezra Soloman, "Alternative Rate of Return Concepts and Their Implications for Utility Regulation", Bell Journal of Economics and Management Science, Spring 1970, pp. 78-79.

28. Survey of Current Business, op. cit.

29. A. E. Scaperlanda and L. J. Mayer, op cit., p. 564.

30. Ibid., p. 565.

31. Op. cit.

32. The S & M figures for changes in book value of U.S. direct investment in the EEC were apparently taken from the same Department of Commerce figures as were those in this study. The S & M figures for the nine-year period 1958-66 (expressed in millions of dollars) were 228, 300, 436 460, 618, 770, 908, 906 and 1283. The figures used in this study for the same time period were 353, 286, 450, 397, 630, 800, 927, 856 and 1330. The differences were particularly large in 1958 (228 vs. 353), 1961 (460 vs. 397), 1965 (906 vs. 856), and 1966 (1283 vs. 1330). See Scaperlanda and Mayer, op. cit., p. 567 and Survey of Current Business, op. cit.

33. Arthur S. Goldberger, Econometric Theory (New York, London, and Sydney: 1964), pp. 236-38.

Adler, Hans A. Economic Appraisal of Transport Projects. Bloomington: Indiana University Press, 1971.

American Economic Association and Royal Economic Society. Surveys
of Economic Theory. Vols. II and III. New York: MacMillan,
1966.

Arthur Anderson & Company. A Tax and Trade Guide to Belgium.
New York, 1967.

Balassa, B. Trade Liberalization Among Industrial Countries. New
York: McGraw-Hill, 1967.

Banca Commerciale Italiana. Vade-Mecum for Foreign Investors in
Italy. Milan, 1968.

Banque de Bruxelles. Belgium—Land of Investments. Brussels, 1965.

Belgian Ministry of Economic Affairs. Industrial Investment in
Belgium—A Practical Guide. Brussels, 1968.

_____. L'Economie Belge en 1968, 1970. Brussels.

_____. L'Investissement Etranger en Belgique. Brussels, 1967,
1968, 1969, and 1970 reports.

Bertin, G. Y. L'Investissement International. Paris: Presses Universitaires de France. 1967.

Bierman, H. Jr., and S. Smidt. The Capital Budgeting Decision.
New York: MacMillan, 1971.

Center for Studies in Vocational and Technical Education, University
of Wisconsin, Madison, and the Industrial Relations, Centre,
Queens University, Kingston, Ontario. Cost-Benefit Analysis
of Manpower Policies. Proceedings of a North American Conference, 1969.

Chase, C. I. Elementary Statistical Procedures, 1967.

Chu, Kong. Principles of Econometrics. Scranton: International
    Textbook, 1968.

Conference Board. Obstacles and Incentives to Private Foreign
    Investment, 1967-68. Vol. II. Studies in Business policy, No.
    130. New York, 1969.

Cooper, Richard N. The Economics of Interdependence: Economic
    Policy in the Atlantic Community. New York: McGraw-Hill
    Paperbacks, 1968.

Denison, E. F. Why Growth Rates Differ. Washington, D.C.: Brookings
    Institution, 1967.

Draper, N. R., and H. Smith. Applied Regression Analysis. New York:
    John Wiley, 1966.

Due, J. F., and R. W. Clower. Intermediate Economic Analysis. Home-
    wood, Ill.: Richard D. Irwin, 1961.

Fellner, W., F. Machlup, and R. Triffin. Maintaining and Restoring
    the Balance of Payments. Princeton, N.J.: Princeton University
    Press, 1966.

Gervais, J. La France Face Aux Investissements Etrangers. Paris:
    Les Editions de l'Entreprise Moderne, 1963.

Goldberger, Arthur S. Econometric Theory. New York: John Wiley,
    1964.

Halm, G. N. The Economics of Money and Banking. Homewood, Ill.:
    Richard D. Irwin, 1962.

Henderson, J. M. and R. E. Quandt. Microeconomic Theory. New York:
    McGraw-Hill, 1958.

Hogan, William T. Depreciation Reform and Capital Replacement.
    Washington, D.C.: American Enterprise Institute, September,
    1962.

Hollander, Jacques. Les Investissements Americains en Belgique.
    Brussels: Editions du Centre Paul Hymans, 1963.

Humphrey, Don D. The United States and the Common Market. New
    York: Praeger, 1964.

Hunt, Pearson; Williams, Charles M.; and Donaldson. Gordon; Basic
    Business Finance. Homewood, Ill.: Richard D. Irwin, 1966.

Isard, Walter. Methods of Regional Analysis. Cambridge, Mass.:
    MIT Press, 1960.

Johnson, Harry G. Economic Policies Toward Less Developed Coun-
    tries. New York: Praeger, 1967.

Johnstone, Allan W. United States Direct Investment in France.
    Cambridge, Mass.: MIT Press, 1965.

Kindleberger, Charles P. American Business Abroad: Six Lectures
    in Direct Investment. New Haven, Conn.: Yale University Press,
    1969.

Klaassen, L. H. Area Economic and Social Development. Paris:
    Organization for Economic Cooperation and Development, 1965.

Kredietbank. Belgium—Key to the Common Market. Brussels, 1966.

Lamfalussy, Alexandre. Investment and Growth in Mature Economies:
    The Case of Belgium. New York: MacMillan, 1961.

Layton, Christopher. L'Europe et les Investissements Americains.
    Paris: Gallimard, 1968 (in English, Trans Atlantic Investments).
    Paris: Atlantic Institute, 1967.

Levitan, Sar. Experiment on Trial. Baltimore: Johns Hopkins Uni-
    versity Press, 1967.

Litvak, Isaiah A., and Christopher J. Maule. Foreign Investment:
    The Experience of Host Countries. New York: Praeger Pub-
    lishers, 1970.

Machlup, F. International Monetary Economics. London: George
    Allen and Unwin, 1964.

Miernyk, W. H. The Elements of Input-Output Analysis. New York:
    Random House, 1969.

Morgan Guaranty Bank and Trust Company. Financing Business in
    Belgium. New York, 1968.

Mundell, Robert A. International Economics. Macmillan, New York:
    1968.

Nourse, H. O. Regional Economics. New York: McGraw-Hill, 1968.

Organization for Economic Cooperation and Development. The Regional
     Factor in Economic Development. Paris: OECD, 1970.

Parl, B. Basic Statistics. New York: Doubleday, 1967.

Postan, M. M. An Economic History of Western Europe, 1945-1964.
     London: Macmillan, 1967.

Potterfield, J. T. S. Investment Decisions and Capital Costs. Engle-
     wood Cliffs, N.J.: Prentice-Hall, 1965.

Rertlinger, Shlomo. Techniques for Project Appaisal under Uncertainty.
     World Bank Staff Occasional Paper. No. 10. Baltimore: Johns
     Hopkins University Press, 1970.

Robert Morris Associates. Annual Statement Studies, 1969 Edition
     for National Association of Bank Loan and Credit Officers,
     (Philadelphia: Robert Morris Associates, 1969).

Robichek, A. A. and S. C. Myers. Optimal Financing Decisions.
     Englewood Cliffs, N.J.: Prentice-Hall, 1965.

Schnitzer, Martin. The Swedish Investment Reserve: A Device for
     Stabilization. Washington, D.C.: American Enterprise Institute,
     July, 1967.

Scitovsky, T. Economic Theory and Western European Integration.
     Stanford, Calif.: Stanford University Press, 1968.

Scott, Ira O. European Capital Markets. New York: McGraw-Hill,
     1968.

Servan-Schreiber, J.-J. Le Defi Americain. Paris: Denoel, 1967.

Societe General de Banque. Industrial Investment in Belgium.
     Brussels, 1967.

Spiller, E. A. Financial Accounting. Homewood, Ill.: Richard D.
     Irwin, 1966.

Tugendhat, C. Oil: The Biggest Business. London: Eyre and
     Spottiswoode, 1968.

Williams, J. R. International Report on Factors in Investment Behavior. Paris: OECD, 1962.

Zenoff, D. B. and J. Zwick, International Financial Management. Englewood Cliffs, N.J.: Prentice-Hall, 1969.

PUBLICATIONS

L'Echo de la Bourse, Brussels.

The Economist, London.

The Economist Intelligence Unit. No. 2 (1970), Singapore-Malaysia.

First National City Bank, New York. Monthly Economic Letters.

Fortune Magazine, issues containing articles on 500 largest U.S. corporations, 1958-71.

Institut National de Statistique. Bulletin de Statistique. Brussels.

International Monetary Fund. Directions of Trade. Washington, D.C.

_____. International Financial Statistics.

Kredietbank. Kredietbank Weekly Bulletin. Brussels.

National Bank of Belgium. Bulletin de l'Information et de Documentation. Brussels.

Organization for Economic Cooperation and Development. OECD Historical Economic Indicators. Paris: OECD, 1965.

_____. OECD Country Reports, published annually by country, Paris: OECD.

Standard and Poor. Standard and Poor's Trade and Securities Index, 1971 New York United Nations. United Nations Statistical Yearbooks. New York.

U.S. Department of Commerce. Survey of Current Business. Washington, D.C.

ARTICLES AND SPEECHES

Alonso, W. "Location Theory," In J. Freedman and W. Alonzo, eds., Regional Development and Planning: A Reader. Cambridge, Mass.: MIT Press, 1964, pp. 78-106.

Bandera, V. N. and White. "U.S. Direct Investments and Domestic Markets in Europe." Economia International, August, 1968.

Barow, J. "La Place des Constructeurs Americans en Europe." Enterprise, No. 369 (October 6, 1952), Paris.

Baumol, W. J. "On the Social Rate of Discount." American Economic Review, September, 1968, pp. 788-802.

Belgian Ministry of Economic Affairs. "Summary of Incentives to Foreign Investment." Brussels, 1968.

Bokanowski, M. M. "Une Politique Concerter de l'investissement en Europe." l'Economie, No. 963 (June 4, 1965), Paris.

Borts, G. H. "Equalization of Returns." American Economic Review, June 1960, pp. 319-47.

Brauers, W. K., "De Opstelling van ein Input-Output Tabel voor de Belgishe Economie in 1958." Cahiers Economiques de Bruxelles, No. 11, 1st Trimester, 1964.

Bridges, B. Jr. "State and Local Inducements for Industry." National Tax Journal, 21, no. 2 (June, 1968), 183-89.

Buchanan, James M. and Moses, John E. "A Regional Countermeasure to National Wage Standardization." American Economic Review, June, 1960, pp. 434-38.

Carnoy, Guy de. "Les Investissements Americans en Europe." L'Europe en Formation, No. 3 (June, 1965), Paris.

Chenery, H. B. "Development Policies for Southern Italy." Quarterly Journal of Economics, Vol. 76 (1962), pp. 515-47.

"Direct U.S. Investment in Europe—A Controversial Issue." European Trends, No. 3 (April, 1965), London.

Due, John F. "Studies of State-Local Tax Influence on the Location
    of Industry." National Tax Journal, 14, no. 2 (June, 1961),
    167-73.

"EEC Is Not Forgetting Its Problem Areas—Sometimes Foreign Invest-
    ment Is Very Welcome." Common Market, Devanter, 8, no. 8
    (1965).

"Enterprises Américaines et Europeenes—Elements de Comparision."
    Patronat Francais, No. 243 (August-September, 1964), Paris.

European Economic Community, "Tableaux Entree-Sortie pour less
    pays de la CEE." Statistical Office for the EEC, October, 1964,
    Paris.

"L'Evaluation des Investissements Americains en Europe." Opera
    Mundi Europe, No. 219 (September 26, 1963), Paris.

Farnsworth, Clyde. "Europeans Facing a Dollar Shortage." New York
    Times, March 5, 1969, p. 51.

Gold, Ronald B. "Subsidies to Industry in Pennsylvania." National
    Tax Journal, 19, no. 3 (September, 1966), 286-97.

Hale, Carl W. "The Optimality of Local Subsidies in Regional Develop-
    ment Programs." Quarterly Review of Business & Economics
    Autumn, 1969, pp. 35-50.

Hertz, David B. "Risk Analysis in Capital Investment." Harvard
    Business Review, January-February 1964.

Houser, J. W., "The Delicate Job of American Management Abroad."
    Advanced Management Office Executive, January, 1962.

"How powerful Is American Industrial Power?" Common Market,
    Devanter, 5, no. 3 (March, 1965).

Humphrey, Don D. "Some Implications of Planning for Trade and
    Capital Movements." Paper presented at A Conference of the
    Universities—National Bureau Committee for Economic Research,
    National Bureau of Economic Research, New York: Columbia
    University Press, 1967, pp. 153-99.

Hymer, Stephen. "The International Operations of National Firms:
    A Study of Direct Investment." Unpublished Doctoral dissertation,
    Cambridge, Mass., MIT, 1960.

"Les Investissements Americains en Europe, Comment sont-ils
    Accueillis en Fait?" L'Economie, No. 948 (February 12, 1965),
    Paris.

"Investissements Americains en Europe, Deaux Prises de Position de
    Grands Industriels Allemandes." Enterprise, No. 503 (April 30,
    1965), Paris.

Jorgeusen D. W. and C. D. Siebert. "A Comparison of Alternative
    Theories of Corporate Investment Behavior." American Economic
    Review, September 1968.

Joy, S. "Railway Track Costs." In Denys Munby, ed., Transport.
    Middlesex: Penguin Modern Economics Series, 1968, pp. 130-49.

Levin, C. L. "Regional and Inter-Regional Accounts in Perspective."
    Papers and Proceedings of the Regional Science Association,
    Vol. 13 (1964).

Lousberg, Philippe. "La Participation Americain à l'Industrie Ali-
    mentaire Belge." L'Echo de la Bourse (Brussels), November
    30, 1967.

Marchand, Jean, "Incentives for Regional Economic Expansion."
    Remarks relating to the introduction of the Regional Develop-
    ment Incentives Bill to the Canadian House of Parliament, May
    27, 1969.

Metzler, L. A. "A Multiple Region Theory of Income and Trade."
    Econometrica, October, 1950, pp. 329-54.

Meyer, J. R., "Regional Economics: A Survey." American Economic
    Review, Vol. 53 (1963), pp. 19-54.

Moulinier, J. "Les Investissements Americains en Europe." Reveu de
    l'Action Politique, No. 190 (July-August, 1965), Paris.

Mundell, Robert A. "International Trade and Factor Mobility."
    American Economic Review, June, 1957.

Nein, J. "Les Investissements Americains dans la Marche Commun."
    Les Problemes de l'Europe, No. 23, 1st Trimester, 1964, Rome-
    Paris.

Nouyrit, H., "Les Investissements U.S. au Europe: Ce qu'enpense la
    Commission de la CEE." L'Economie, No. 957 (April 23, 1967),
    Paris.

"Overseas Investment." Business Week, No. 1723 (September 8, 1962),
    New York.

"Regional Development Incentive Act and the Regional Development
    Incentives Regulations." Canadian House of Parliament, Bill
    passed July 9, 1969. Ottawa: Queen's Printer for Canada, 1969.

Ross, S. R. and J. H. Guttentag, "United States Taxation of International
    Business Transactions." In W. S. Surrey and C. Shaw, eds.,
    A Lawyer's Guide to International Business Transactions.
    Philadelphia: Joint Committee on Continuing Legal Education
    of the American Law Institute and the American Bar Association,
    1963, pp. 719-840.

Scaperlanda, Anthony E. and Mauer, Laurence J. "Determinants of
    U.S. Direct Investment in the EEC," American Economic Review,
    September, 1969.

Schmitt, Peter G. "Le Comportement d'un Investisseur Americain a
    l'egarde du Marche Commun." Opera Mundi Europe, No. 103
    (May 11, 1961), Paris.

Segre, C. "Capital Movements in the European Economic Community."
    Quarterly Review (Banco Nazionale del Lavoro), No. 60 (March,
    1962), Rome.

Societe General de Banque. "Government Aid for Investment in
    Belgium." 1968, Brussels.

Societe Nationale de Credit a l'Industrie. "Credit a l'Industrie."
    1968, Brussels.

Soloman, Ezra. "Alternative Rate of Return Concepts and their Impli-
    cations for Utility Regulation." Bell Journal of Economics and
    Management Science, Spring, 1970.

Stobaugh, Robert B. A. Jr., "How to Analyze Foreign Investment
    Climates." Harvard Business Review, September-October, 1969.

_____. "Where in the World Shall We Put That Plant." Harvard
    Business Review, January-February, 1969, pp. 124-36.

Tilot, J. A. "Les Investissements Americains en Belgique et la
     Cooperation Industrielle Belgo-Americaine en vue du Marche
     Commun." Bulletin Commercial Belge, No. 4 (April, 1961),
     Brussels.

Turot, Paul. "Les Societies Americains a la Decouverte de l'Europe."
     Revue Politique et Parliementaire, No. 755 (April, 1965), Paris.

"U.S. Investment Activity in Europe during 1964." Report on Western
     Europe (Chase Manhattan Bank), No. 34 (February-March 1965),
     New York.

Vining, R. "The Region as an Economic Entity and Certain Variations
     to be Observed in the Study of Systems of Regions." Papers
     and Proceedings of the American Economic Association, Vol. 39
     (May, 1969).

Wauters, Luc. Speech before the Belgian-American Chamber of
     Commerce, St. Regis Sheraton Hotel, New York City, September
     29, 1967.

Williamson, J. C. "Regional Inequality and National Development:
     A Description of the Patterns." In W. L. Needleman, ed.,
     Regional Analysis. Middlesex: Penguin Modern Economics
     Series, 1968, pp. 99-158.

G. RICHARD THOMAN is an associate in the New York Office of McKinsey & Company, specializing in problems of international finance. Previously employed by the Treasurer's Departments of Standard Oil Company (New Jersey) and Esso International, Inc., he has considerable experience in the practical aspects of international finance, including evaluating the attractiveness of government subsidy measures to promote foreign investment.

Dr. Thoman received a B.A. (Honors) in economics and political science from McGill University and graduate degrees in international economics and finance from the Graduate Institute of International Studies (Geneva) and the Fletcher School of Law and Diplomacy.